ELDER CARE:
THE ROAD TO GROWING OLD IS NOT PAVED

****

A Comprehensive Reference Guide to Planning for Legal, Financial and Health Care in Later Life

Buckley Fricker, JD, CMC

Elder Care: The Road to Growing Old is Not Paved
Copyright 2015 by Buckley Fricker, JD, CMC
Bellview Publishing

ISBN: 978-1-365-73874-6

This book addresses the "double whammy" facing Baby Boomers: preparing for their own retirement while simultaneously caring for elderly loved ones. It is a reference manual for professionals, family caregivers and those contemplating their own later years, who need both general descriptions and easy-to-find important details about complex aging-related options. It is a guide to help readers and loved ones ensure that their later years turn out how they want them to turn out.

Special thanks to:
Janet L. Kuhn - Contributing Editor
Deb Merriner - Editor
Deb Merriner - Typing Virtuoso
Ginny Hamel and Amanda Babineau - Researchers
Allan Goodman and Bart Astor - Publishing Advisors
My Family - Champion Supporters of My Efforts

PREFACE
How to Use This Book

There are different ways you can take full advantage of what this book has to offer. You can, of course, simply read through it as you would any book. But the book is also designed to provide convenient access for those who have interests in particular elder care topics. Scan the TABLE OF CONTENTS to find desired headings and subheadings. There are two TABLES OF CONTENTS, a short form and a detailed version, which follows it. The first TABLE OF CONTENTS will reflect the major headings of the book; the EXPANDED TABLE OF CONTENTS will give you detailed subheadings for your convenience in locating specific information.

At the back of the book you will find an ACRONYM APPENDIX and GLOSSARY. As is true in almost every field, the world of planning for later life has its own vocabulary. The first time a phrase with an acronym appears, it will be followed by the acronym in parentheses. After the first mention, both the full phrase and the acronym will be sprinkled throughout the text. When in doubt, check the ACRONYM APPENDIX.

This book is intended to be generally applicable throughout the country. Federal matters are, for the most part, consistent across the U.S. However, topics such as estate planning, Medicaid planning, guardianship/conservatorship proceedings and probate procedures can vary significantly from state to state. I use Virginia for examples because that's where I live. The numbers, statistics, and dollar amounts in this book are widely available from many sources.

On the whole, this is a general reference book. It does not attempt to match the multi-inch tomes written *by* lawyers *for* lawyers. Those books are the ones used by the lawyers whom *this* book strongly recommends you retain for "the real thing." There's a reason those professional-to-professional books are very thick and very technical. This book aims to provide a more accessible view of key elder care options.

Planning regarding legal and care issues is very complex. If nothing else, you need a strong understanding of what's out there. This book will help straighten out the differences between and among various programs and choices. It will get you started on the path to learning what opportunities exist for those who are, or will be elderly. This book offers a glimpse into your own later years, and is intended to be useful to both caregivers and professionals. It should also help you to decide when you need to seek more information in more depth.

PLEASE NOTE: This book is intended to provide general reference information about specific elder care topics. Most of the information provided reflects the tips of many icebergs in terms of the extensive volume of applicable statutes, regulations, exceptions, exceptions to exceptions, court decisions, as well as federal, state and local practices and procedures and the interactions between and among all of these. Individual circumstances to which this information may apply must be evaluated in terms of those specific individual circumstances. Such more-in-depth evaluations should be conducted in consultation with your elder law and/or estate planning attorney, your financial advisor, your CPA or your Aging Life Care Manager TM, as the case may be.

Nothing contained in this book is intended to be, or should be interpreted as, legal advice.

INTRODUCTION

I wanted to write a book that explains in plain language some of the most complex and emotional issues facing our aging baby boomers today. This book has been evolving for a decade. During that decade, the number of pre-elderly Americans aged 60-64 jumped from 11 million to 17 million. During any given year, more than fifty million Americans serve as unpaid caregivers for elderly or disabled loved ones. Many of these people are concerned about their own futures while simultaneously caring for elderly loved ones.

While working in an elder law firm, I found that I greatly enjoyed interacting with the firm's elderly clients. Clients who lived alone in the community would often call the office because their air conditioning wouldn't work or their power went out. They called us because they had no one else to call. Neighbors they had known for years had died or moved away. They either had out-of-state family or no family at all. Answering their calls and handling their problems became some of my favorite tasks. At the firm I also discovered that the primary work of an elder law attorney involved lots of computations, whether for estate and gift tax purposes or for Medicaid planning purposes. Math is not among my favorite things. I began to realize that I was more inclined to be a surrogate family member for elders than to be their elder law attorney.

In 2005 I founded Buckley's for Seniors, LLC, which provides concierge/companion-type non-healthcare-related services for people who are elderly or disabled. Buckley's provides transportation, whether to doctor appointments or errands or hairdressers. We help get pets to the vet and clients to their favorite restaurants. We are like stand-in adult children with knowledge about caregiving that can be truly helpful to our elderly clients and their families.

We go for walks with our clients. We provide companionship, supervision of home maintenance, grocery shopping, assistance with moving and myriad other needs - needs that would ideally be handled by loving adult children who could respond to mom's or dad's concerns at a moment's notice but who live too far away to handle these tasks. We help our clients and their families choose paid home caregivers. We help them choose where they would want to live if staying at home becomes unsafe or financially impracticable.

Along the way, I became an Advanced Aging Life Care Manager TM. (see www.aginglifecare.org). In due course, I began teaching a retirement and elder care class at a local community college. This book grew out of those classes. It is a primer on the broad range of elder care issues that my students said they considered invaluable. They urged me to convert my class to a book. This is that book.

Do you know the difference between Medicare and Medicaid?

~

Is it true that Medicare does not cover most nursing home costs?

~

Can my ex really get Social Security benefits based on my work record if I am re-married?

~

My Dad shouldn't be driving or living alone. What are the options?

~

A relative wants me to be her Power of Attorney. What does that mean?

~

FIND ANSWERS TO THESE IMPORTANT QUESTIONS AND MORE IN THE PAGES THAT FOLLOW!

TABLE OF CONTENTS

EXPANDED

TABLE OF CONTENTS

****

MEDICARE

Medicare is a government-run health insurance plan that was created in 1965 to cover older Americans who would otherwise find it very difficult to obtain private health insurance coverage because of age-related illnesses and pre-existing conditions. (Health Insurance Companies don't usually profit from the 65+ crowd). It is insurance for health care most people receive because they paid for it through payroll taxes. The program is run by the Centers for Medicare and Medicaid Services (CMS), an agency of the Social Security Administration. Statements that come in the mail have the CMS logo on them. In 1972, Medicare was expanded to cover other groups of people under age 65 such as those who have End-Stage Renal Disease (ESRD) and Lou Gehrig's Disease (ALS). Additionally, those who are receiving Social Security Disability Income (SSDI) may begin to receive Medicare after a 24-month waiting period.

Medicare now has an online service called "Blue Button:" http://bluebuttonconnector.healthit.gov . The Medicare website states that individuals can use the tool for:

- Reference - your health records to be reminded when you had your last shot, or the exact date of a procedure.

- Check - the accuracy of your records, monitor changes, and stay aware of your health status.

- Share - with your doctor or someone else you trust, when traveling, seeking a second opinion, moving, switching insurance, or in case of emergency.

- Use Apps to help better manage and coordinate your healthcare to achieve your health goals.

You can think of the Lettered Parts of Medicare as Fruit.
You either have Traditional Medicare (Parts A, B, D and if you choose, Medigap OR you have Part C (combines A, B, D and Medigap into one plan).

Parts A, B, D and Medigap are like 4 grapes in a bunch consisting of 4 grapes.
Part C is like an apple.

This is the reason the for the order of the Medicare Parts explained below. The letters are not "out of order" so to speak. The explanation of how Medicare works would not be clear if I talked about 3 of the grapes, then the apple, and then another grape.

Part A: Hospitalization, Hospice, Skilled Nursing and Rehabilitation

Medicare Part A hospital insurance is primarily funded through payroll taxes. Individuals can enroll during the initial enrollment period, three months before and three months after their 65th birthday, or later on, during the annual enrollment period, January 1 through March 31 each year. There is no penalty for late enrollment as long as you have 40 work credits (see "work credits" in Social Security section). If you have earned 40 credits, there is no monthly premium for Part A because you already "bought it" over many years of payroll taxes. If you have not earned 40 credits by the time you are age 65, you can purchase Part A for a monthly premium that depends on the number of Social Security work credits you have earned. Each year a new premium amount may be published depending on whether the Cost of Living Adjustment (COLA) goes up.

In 2017, individuals with 30 to 39 Social Security credits will pay a monthly premium for Medicare Part A of $226. Individuals with fewer than 30 Social Security credits will pay $411 a month in premiums. Those who cannot afford those premiums may qualify to have payment assistance through Medicaid, a separate federal program also run by CMS.

If you have fewer than 40 credits and you *apply late* for Medicare, you may have to pay a surcharge of 10% of the current Part A premium amount. In 2017, the maximum premium is $411. Therefore, the annual surcharge would be about $41, distributed evenly throughout the year. The penalty surcharge continues for *twice* the number of years that enrollment was delayed.

Hospital costs can be so high, that Medicare really wants you to purchase Part A if you are not already getting for no premium. A lot of hospital costs never get paid and the cost is absorbed eventually by those paying for insurance and care. The penalty is meant to motivate people to purchase the plan, to save them from potentially huge hospital bills and to defray the cost to the system of unpaid bills of the un-insured.

NOTE: If you are a dependent of a Primary Worker with 40 credits, you do not have to pay a Part A premium.

If you are already receiving or have signed up for Social Security retirement benefits you will *automatically* be enrolled in Medicare Part A when you turn 65. Those who have not signed up for Social Security by age 65 must enroll between *three months before and three months after* the month in which they turn 65. If you apply before your birthday, coverage will then begin on the first day of your birth month. You can also enroll in Medicare within the three months after you turn 65 but that will result in some delayed coverage, up to a few months.

If you do not sign up for Medicare Part A within the enrollment period, three months before and three months after your 65th birthday, or you are not automatically enrolled because you are receiving Social Security by the time you are 65, you may still do so by contacting the Social Security Administration. However, you can only enroll during the specified enrollment period between January 1 and March 31 of each year. Those who enroll during this "open" enrollment period must wait until July 1 for coverage to begin.

Part A - Out-of-Pocket Costs 2017 Figures

Although Medicare Part A coverage for most people will not require payment of a monthly premium, Part A coverage does require payment of an initial deductible and subsequent coinsurance amounts paid to hospitals and skilled nursing facilities (SNFs) and/or rehabilitation centers. Note: Supplemental Medicare insurance, or "Medigap," may cover some or all of the following out-of-pocket costs (as discussed later).

Days 1 through 60 of a hospital stay incur a one-time deductible of $1,288 and no co-pay. *Days 61 through 90* incur a $322 per day coinsurance charge paid to the hospital.

These out-of-pocket costs are owed each time an individual experiences hospitalization for up to 90 days; this is known as a "spell of illness." However, for each spell of illness to be considered a separate benefit period, there must an at least 60-day "period of wellness" between hospital stays. Coverage for up to 90 days is called a "benefit period." There is no limit to the number of benefit periods you can have. If the hospital stays are fewer than 60 days apart, the out-of-pocket costs will simply start on whatever day of the hospital stay you left off on during your prior hospitalization. Each stay up to 90 days in a hospital *could exceed* $9000 in out-of-pocket expenses if you have *no supplemental insurance* (i.e., Medigap).

Days 91 through 150 will cost you a co-insurance payment of $644 per day. Days 91 through 150 are called "Lifetime Reserve Days." The part that Medicare covers for days 91 through 150 cannot be renewed each time you have a new hospitalization at least 60 days apart. Medicare covers nothing for hospital stays 150 days and beyond. However, it is rare for anyone to remain hospitalized for more than 90 days because skilled nursing facilities (SNFs) and rehabilitation centers can now provide the kind of skilled care that used to be available only in a hospital.

If you have supplemental insurance – "Medigap" – most of the out-of-pocket costs will be paid for by the policy. However, there are several variations of these policies, (see section on Medigap policies, below).

Skilled Nursing Care and Rehabilitation 2017 Figures

A skilled nursing facility (SNF) is certified by the CMS to provide skilled care and rehabilitation that is covered by Medicare if you meet certain qualifications. In order to qualify for Medicare coverage in a SNF, you must meet the following requirements:

- a physician's certification that you need skilled nursing care or rehabilitation on a daily basis;
- inpatient hospital stay for three days prior to transferring to a skilled care facility (called the "Three-Day Rule"); and,
- admittance to the SNF within 30 days of the hospitalization for the same illness or injury.

For each benefit period: *Days 1 through 20* of SNF or rehabilitation care require no out-of-pocket costs.

Days 21 through 100 have a $161.00 per day co-pay. The full cost of *days 101 and beyond* is charged to the patient. Again, Medigap insurance will cover all or part of these co-pays.

Regarding the "Three-Day Rule," a caution: even if you are kept overnight in the emergency room (ER) of a hospital, or even a regular hospital room, that stay may not necessarily count toward the three-day minimum "hospital inpatient admission" prerequisite for Medicare Part A coverage. Patients who remain in the hospital over a three-day period "for observation" are not considered to have met the three-day Part A requirement. Therefore, you could be shocked to find that Medicare will not cover your SNF costs if you have been in a hospital for three days. You or your representative must verify whether or not you have officially been "admitted" for inpatient services at the hospital itself.

If you stop getting skilled care in a SNF, for a period that lasts more than 30 days, a new day three-day inpatient hospital stay will be required for additional SNF care. If the break in skilled care lasts for at least 60 days in a row, the old benefit period will cease and a new benefit period will begin, starting with the coinsurance fees listed above for Days 1 through 100. The new hospital stay does not have to be for the same condition.

Inpatient Psychiatric Care

Medicare Part A also includes *Inpatient Psychiatric Care* coverage for 190 days with the same fees as those for regular hospitalization. However, all 190 days are counted as "Lifetime Reserve Days" (as discussed above) and cannot be renewed.

This applies to Psychiatric Hospitals and not inpatient psychiatric services in General Hospitals.

Note: There may be additional copays due for mental health services from doctors and other providers at the hospital. The copay amount is 20%.

Hospice

Part A covers doctors, registered nurses (RNs), and medications for pain control and palliative care. (See later section entitled Hospice). Part A also covers certain durable medical equipment such as a wheel chair or hospital bed, and spiritual or grief counseling. Hospice care provided in a Hospice facility is 100% covered by Medicare Part A.

However, most hospice patients are cared for in their own homes where a family member, friend or paid home health aide (HHA) is the primary caregiver. Part A will also pay for some *respite care*, such as services provided by a home health aide to allow a break for the family member or other friend who usually provides regular non-skilled care. Respite care can include limited homemaker services. In some cases, the patient can be moved to an inpatient facility for up to five days to provide respite care for the primary caregiver.

This means you still have to pay for your housing costs such as the Assisted Living or Nursing Home fees if you are not in your own home, just like people who live at home pay their rent or mortgage.

To qualify for Medicare *hospice coverage*, the patient's life expectancy must be certified by a physician to be fewer than six months. If a patient lives more than six months, the hospice care period can be renewed by a physician.

Medicare In-Home Care Coverage

Medicare Part A provides coverage for some medical care *in your own home*. Typically, in-home service-coverage occurs after a three-day hospital admission, or upon discharge from a skilled nursing facility. Medicare pays for physical, occupational and speech therapists, depending on the need, as well as RN visits to provide services such as wound care and medication management. Generally, Medicare does not cover the costs of a home health aide to assist with personal care and activities of daily living (ADLs) or supervision. However, during these covered periods, Medicare will pay for a home health aide to come a few times a week for short periods of time to assist with certain activities of daily living such as personal hygiene and grooming, dressing and undressing, self-feeding, transferring (getting in and out of a bed or wheelchair), toileting, and ambulation (walking without an assistive device).

Medicare Part A also offers a Home Health benefit that you don't have to spend 3 days in a hospital before qualifying for. To qualify, you must be generally confined to your home, i.e., housebound, except for short outings such as to a medical appointment. A physician must approve the treatment plan and certify that the care is medically necessary. The certification for the in-home coverage under Part A must be reviewed every 60 days to certify whether there is still need. The in-home care that is covered by Medicare part A must be part-time and/or intermittent and must include the need for skilled nursing care. You won't qualify if you need full-time help, or all you need is help with things such as bathing and dressing. Physical and occupational therapy, speech therapy, medical social services, medical supplies and some assistance from a home health aide will be provided if deemed by a doctor to be medically necessary.

It is important not to confuse the services Medicare may provide in your home, during what is called "an episode of care," with the need for long-term care from a home health aide. The intent of the Medicare benefit is to treat an individual with a condition or illness that has a reasonable expectation of recovery.

Part B: Doctor's Visits, Medical Tests, Outpatient Care, Durable Medical Equipment, Ambulance Services, Preventative Services

The enrollment period is January 1 through March 31 each year (if you didn't sign up around when you turned 65). The premium amount you pay is based on your income. CMS uses your income as stated on your tax return 2 years prior, because most people have gotten those in already and it is a solid official number to base things on. The premium is withheld from your Social Security payment.

Many people are surprised to learn that Part B does *not* cover:

- Routine hearing exams, such as hearing aid exams or hearing aid fittings – exception- a hearing exam if ordered by a doctor to check for a medical condition.

- Dental exams, cleanings, fillings etc. – exception – if you are hospitalized, Part A may cover some necessary dental services, or, will pay for hospitalization for an emergency or complicated procedure even if it is dental-related.

- Routine eye exams- exception- an annual glaucoma screening for people with certain risk factors or an injury to the eye which would fall under Part A or B coverage depending on what kind of treatment is needed.

- Most long-term care costs such as assisted living, nursing home, and home health aides.

Part B has an annual $183 deductible (2017). After that, Medicare Part B will pay 80% of the approved amount for the medical service you receive. You, your supplemental insurance, or Medigap Plan, must cover the rest.

If you delay your enrollment in Part B past your initial enrollment period, you will be required to pay a 10% penalty which will be added to your premium *indefinitely*. This is significantly different from the penalty for delaying Part A, which ends after double the time-period of the delay. Because Part B covers some preventative care and doctor visits, it costs the system more if you do not catch and treat health issues early on. The enrollment period for Part B is the same as for Medicare Part A. If you are enrolled in Social Security, you will automatically start receiving Medicare Part B when you turn 65.

If you are still working at 65 and you have insurance through your work, you can delay enrollment in Part B as long as your insurance is at least as comprehensive as Medicare Part B. Otherwise, a delay in signing up will result in the 10% penalty. Check with CMS to see if your work plan qualifies. If you do not sign up for Part B during the enrollment period surrounding your 65th birthday because you are working and you do not want to pay two premiums, you have eight months to do so after you leave your employer's insurance coverage without incurring the 10% penalty.

If you decide to enroll in Part B while you are still working and have insurance through your work, Part B may function as a *secondary insurance*. That will depend on your employer's discretion and the employer's contract with the insurance company. When you stop working, Part B will become your primary insurance and you may or may not have the option to keep your employment health insurance on as a secondary insurance similar to a Medigap or supplemental policy.

Part B premiums increase as income increases. A chart of all various income groups and resulting premiums is available at www.medicare.gov/pubs/pdf/10050-Medicare-and-You.pdf in the *Medicare and You (official U.S. government handbook for 2017)*.

Medicare Part B premiums are based on your income reported on your tax return two years prior. In 2017:

- For individual incomes up to $85,000 and joint incomes up to $170,000, the premium is $134.00 per month;
- For individual incomes above $85,000 up to $107,000, and joint incomes $170,000 to $214,000, the premium is $187.50;
- For individual incomes above $107,000 up to $160,000, and joint incomes $214,000 to $320,000, the premium is $267.90;
- For individual incomes above $160,000 up to $214,000, and joint incomes $320,000 to $428,000, the premium is $348.30;
- For individual incomes above $214,000, and joint incomes above $428,000, the premium is $428.60.

If you have a hard time affording these part B premiums, you may be eligible to receive help with the cost through your state's assistance program. In this case, you would also qualify for a special Part D drug benefit as well. Contact your local Department of Human Services office for more information.

Medical providers are not required by the government to participate in Medicare. Those who do not accept Medicare can charge any amount they want. Those who do agree to participate in Medicare *may* agree to "accept assignment." Medicare assigns an "approved amount" for care costs. Medicare will pay the medical provider 80% of that "approved amount." If a doctor accepts assignment of those amounts, it means the amount the doctor charges you will be that remaining 20%.

Medical providers may also agree to participate in Medicare billing but not "accept assignment" which means they may bill patients for more than the Medicare allowance but not an unlimited amount. The actual limit is somewhat confusing to calculate but comes out to an approximate ceiling of 15% over the charge that physicians who accept assignment can bill the patient.

Where is Part C? Part C information appears later on in this book. Why?

Traditional Medicare consists of Parts A, B, D and (if you purchase it) Medigap.

Part C includes all of the parts of traditional Medicare wrapped up into one plan.

You either have the A, B, D and Medigap OR you have Part C.

Remember, Traditional Medicare is like a small bunch of grapes made up of four grapes. It is several parts that act together.

Part C is like an apple.

In this book we will first look at the grapes and then later on, the apple, and disregard the confusing letters whose alphabetical designations can make Medicare harder to understand.

Part D: Prescription Drug Benefits

Medicare Part D is a prescription drug benefit plan available since 2006. Part D drug plans are offered *by private insurance companies*. Insurance companies who provide Part D coverage must do so under guidelines set by Medicare, but they are private entities competing to get people to enroll. You will see ads for drug plans everywhere from your local pharmacy to magazines to TV ads.

In 2017 the average base premium for Part D plans is $35.63 a month. If you are paying for Part D in 2017, the amount would be based on your 2015 income. The surcharges on top of the base premium if you owe one based on income amounts are listed below.

- For individual incomes up to $85,000 and joint incomes up to $170,000, the surcharge is $0 month;
- For individual incomes above $85,000 up to $107,000, and joint incomes $170,000 to $214,000, the surcharge is $13.30 per month;
- For individual incomes above $107,000 up to $160,000, and joint incomes $214,000 to $320,000, the surcharge is $34.20;
- For individual incomes above $160,000 up to $214,000, and joint incomes $320,000 to $428,000, the surcharge is $55.20 per month;
- For individual incomes above $214,000, and joint incomes above $428,000, the surcharge is $76.20 per month.

You can find a list of Part D providers at the medicare.gov website and use a prescription drug plan finder with your zip code to find plan comparisons. Similar to real estate taxes, some places are just more expensive to live in than others.

The annual Part D deductible varies by plan, but can be up to a maximum *of* $400 in 2017, after which time the Part D benefit will cover certain medications in certain amounts depending on the plan you choose.

The initial enrollment period for Part D is the same as for other parts of Medicare – October 15 through December 7, and your coverage will begin January 1. You can also enroll in Part D through certain organizations such as AARP, but if you go that route, you will only be offered a plan by their one preferred provider. There are many Part D providers.

If you do not enroll during enrollment times, you may incur a *lifetime penalty* on your Part D premiums. If you delay your enrollment in Part D, Medicare will penalize you 1% of the national base premium amount. For example, in 2017 the "national base beneficiary premium is $35.63 each month, the penalty will be about 35 cents per month. Example: an individual delays enrolling in a Part D plan for 10 months after eligibility. A 1% charge for 10 months results in a 10% penalty on top of the average base premium, rounded down to the nearest $0.10. During 2017, the individual will have to pay $35.63 plus $0.36 each month. The amount of penalty will change each year that the national base premium is changed.

If you receive Medicare due to a disability (through SSDI), you can apply for Medicare Part D from three months before to three months after the 25th month of receipt of disability payments.

Medicare also offers an incentive to switch to a "Five Star Medicare Prescription Drug Plan". Each year Medicare publishes a list of Drug Plans that qualify as having a 5 Star Rating. You will be able to choose to switch once to one of these plans if one is available in your area between December 8 of the current year and November 30 of the following year. The enrollment times may be subject to change each year.

Exceptions to these enrollment period rules include but may not be limited to:

- You move out of your Part D Plan's service area
- You move to a facility, like a nursing home in your area, that doesn't participate in the Plan D you had been enrolled in
- You enroll within seven months of becoming uncovered by a similar qualifying drug plan through your employer
- You enroll within 63 days of becoming uncovered by another Medicare Part D provider
- Your income and resources are below a threshold and you need to utilize the Medicare "Extra Help" program, which will enroll you in original Medicare and help cover costs like premiums, deductibles, coinsurance and copayment costs.

For the year 2017, Part D beneficiaries are covered for prescriptions costs up to $3700. At that point, the **"donut hole"** begins. The donut hole is a partial gap in prescription coverage that begins when total prescription costs equal $3,700. The "total" cost is what you pay, plus the part of the drug cost that your plan covers. The gap continues until your total out-of-pocket prescription costs minus gap coverage, which varies for generic versus non-generic drugs, equal $4,950 in 2017. (The donut hole for 2017 spans $1250.) After total prescription costs equal $4950, you will emerge from the donut hole. At that point, "catastrophic coverage" kicks in and a small co-payment will apply to your prescription drug costs with amounts depending on your plan. Each year these amounts restart.

NOTE: The cost of drugs you may decide to purchase anyway, that are not "covered" at all by your plan, do not count for the purposes of these donut hole figures.

Part D supplemental policies can cover much or most of the costs of prescriptions you purchase while you are in the donut-hole gap. With plan coverage, in 2017, you will pay no more than 51% of the price for generic drugs and 40% of the price for name brand medication costs purchased within the donut hole. However, the full retail price of the drugs, regardless of your discounts, will be applied toward reaching the amount that will get you out of the donut hole. While you're in the donut hole, a bunch of really confusing dollar amounts and percentages (which change each year) are used to calculate: a) how much you actually pay the pharmacist for the medication and b) what complex dollar amount Medicare has calculated the drug to represent inside the donut hole. For example, you pay the pharmacist $25 for your medication. Medicare implements a complicated equation that generally has to do with percentages of the drug cost, dispensing fees, manufacturers' discount payments, etc. That number comes out to $60. It is the $60-dollar amount that Medicare applies to the $1250.

It is important to read notices that come in from your Part D provider. They can decide to not cover certain medications, and if it is one you need, you may want to shop around for a new plan.

For low income beneficiaries, the Part D Extra Help Program can be valuable. Call 1-800-772-1213 for more information. Or visit www.socialsecurity.gov/extrahelp.

The Donut Hole will get smaller, bottoming out at a drug cost of 25% for all drugs in the donut hole in the year 2020.

Medication Therapy Management (MTM Program)

Individuals who take several different medications, or who have chronic health conditions or who have very high drug costs may benefit from Medication Therapy Management. This MTM Program option offers you a pharmacist or other healthcare professional to do a comprehensive review of your medications, address any questions or concerns you may have, note possible interactions with over-the-counter medications you take, etc. and provide you with a written summary.

Medicare suggests you schedule your "annual wellness exam" after you have a chance to participate in the MTM Program so you can take the summary sheet with you to your doctor to discuss if any changes should be made.

MEDIGAP, AKA SUPPLEMENTAL INSURANCE: PRIVATE INSURANCE TO FILL IN THE GAPS OF TRADITIONAL MEDICARE

Medigap Overview

Medicare supplemental insurance, also called Medigap, is a type of policy you can purchase separately that can help you with the co-payments and deductibles not covered by Medicare. These plans are offered by *private insurance companies*. There are many options available. You can compare Medigap policies at www.medicare.gov. The plans are standardized by CMS.

If you work, it may be possible to convert your current employee insurance plan to your Medigap policy once you retire. If you do not have the opportunity to keep an employer plan as a Medigap policy after you retire, or don't want to, you can buy a policy, but important time restrictions apply. Different plans are offered in different parts of the country. Do a Google-type search for "Medigap" and the "name of your state" to find comparisons of the various plans available to you or check www.cms.gov.

The Medigap enrollment period is *six months* from the first day of the month in which you turn 65. To purchase Medigap insurance you must be enrolled in Medicare Part B. *This time period is very important*: if you enroll during this enrollment period, the insurance company cannot use *medical underwriting* to deny you for "pre-existing conditions." If you change Medigap policies, you must do so within 63 days in order to avoid underwriting.

Medigap policies cover expenses left over from what your Medicare plan has paid, such as annual co-pays and deductibles. Note: you cannot purchase a Medigap policy if you have Medicare Part C, because Medicare Part C Advantage plans already include their own Medigap-type coverage.

Medigap Policies

Medigap Policies are differentiated from one another by letters. Some policy letters are no longer available for purchase, but are still effective if you have one. The CMS states that current plans available for purchase are titled: A, B, C, D, F, G, K, L, M and N. <u>Note: Medigap Plans A through D are *not the same* as Medicare Parts A through D; do not get confused and think that if you have Medicare Parts A, B, C or D that you also have a Medigap Plan of the same letter.</u> Each plan offers different benefits, for different costs,

(costs can depend on the area of the country in which you live), depending on what additional coverage you feel you need to supplement the coverage Medicare provides you. For instance, all of the ten options have a benefit for Medicare Part A hospital coinsurance for stays up to an additional 365 days after Medicare is used up.

It is generally felt that Plans F, G and C are the most comprehensive Medigap plans available for purchase. For instance, Plan F covers 100% of the gaps in Medicare coverage including paying for your Medicare Part B deductible. Plan G covers 100% of the gaps but you must still pay the Medicare Part B deductible. Plans C, D, F, G, M and N have Foreign Travel Emergency coverage options. Plans A and B, for example, do not have any coverage for skilled nursing care coinsurance. The rest of the lettered plans provide varying coverage for those costs ranging from 50% to 100% for skilled nursing care.

There is also what is called a "High Deductible Plan F". Instead of the most expensive monthly premiums for traditional Part F, you pay much lower monthly fees, but have to pay out of pocket up to $2,020 before the benefits kick in. For those who feel fairly healthy and may feel a monthly premium is not necessary in their case because they won't use the benefit, the High Deductible Plan F can act like a "catastrophic coverage" safety net, just in case.

www.medicare.gov provides a chart showing all of the ten lettered plan options and what each one covers. Because the costs for these plans vary by state and insurance company provider, you will have to check with local companies to determine the premiums for each Medigap-lettered option in your area.

Part C: Everything in One Package - aka MEDICARE ADVANTAGE

Part C is offered through private, for profit health insurance companies, who usually use advertising to get members. That is why they came up with the catchy name using the term "Medicare Advantage".

Medicare Part C is an alternative to the combination of Parts A, B, D, and a Medigap or other supplemental policy. Part C is offered by private insurance companies. With Part C coverage, you receive almost all your health care in "one-stop shopping" in the way that an HMO operates for regular health insurance. If you opt for Part C, your monthly payment covers what you would have been purchasing separately as Parts A, B, D and Medigap. However, you are limited in your choice of doctors and pharmacies. Part C plans offer a reduction in your overall cost in exchange for a narrower choice of providers.

The initial enrollment period for Part C is the same as for Parts A and B, during the six months surrounding your 65th birthday. If you do not enroll during the initial enrollment period, (three months before and three months after your 65th birthday), the enrollment period is from October 15th through December 7th of each year. If you decide to leave a Part C plan and go back to original Medicare, there is a special additional period only for leaving a Plan C to join original Medicare: between January 1st and February 14th. However, you are required to sign up for a Part D drug plan during this period as well. Your new original Medicare plan will begin on the first day of the month after your enrollment request is received.

There are exceptions to these enrollment/change policy periods including but not limited to:

- You move out of your Part C Plan's service area
- You move to a facility, like a nursing home in your area, that provides services under original Medicare (A, B and D)
- Your income and resources are below a threshold and you need to utilize the Medicare "Extra Help" program, which will enroll you in original Medicare (A, B and D), and help cover costs like premiums, deductibles, coinsurance and copayment costs.

LONG-TERM CARE INSURANCE (LTCI)

LTCI Overview

Only about 5% of long-term care (LTC) nursing home costs are considered "medical" or "skilled" care covered by Medicare. The patient is responsible, one way or another, for the remaining 95%. The average cost of a nursing home for a semi-private room is roughly $87,000 annually. Some patients can afford private-pay nursing home costs from their own resources. Some patients' care is covered by generous family members. Most patients' long-term care costs (about 68%) are covered by Medicaid because they have run out of money to pay for their care and must rely on state funding.

For illnesses, such as Alzheimer's Disease or damage from a severe stroke, needed care is usually "unskilled" or "custodial" care provided by home health aides or certified nursing assistants (CNAs). Therefore, it is not covered by Medicare or Medigap.

Long-term care insurance is privately purchased insurance that helps to cover some or all long-term care expenses. It is especially appropriate for those who would *almost* be able to cover their own costs of care, but would be very financially stressed doing so.

Long-term care insurance policies have many options. Today's policies routinely cover not only nursing home care, but also care in assisted living facilities (ALFs) or in your own home. Long-term care insurance can consist of stand-alone policies; others combine both long-term care benefits and death benefits. The younger and healthier you are, the better the chances are you'll be able to purchase a long-term care insurance plan. As is usually true of life insurance policies, LTC plan providers may use underwriting (examining your medical history and pre-existing conditions) to establish eligibility. In order for actual long-term care insurance payments to begin under most policies, you must either have been diagnosed with a dementing illness or exhibit deficiencies in at least two Activities of Daily Living (ADLs).

There is a long list of conditions that will make you automatically uninsurable. Generally speaking, if there are any serious illnesses for which you are already being treated or for which you need or foreseeably might need custodial help, you will probably be found uninsurable. Nevertheless, insurance companies do not all follow the same policies. One company's "denial" may be another's "standard risk" that will simply raise the premium rate, but still offer coverage.

Long-term care insurance policies have evolved significantly over the years. Your parents' policy may look quite different from what is being offered today. Available options for LTC policies can be very complicated and affect the price of the policy.

Some of the main variables to consider when discussing options with a financial or insurance expert are:

- benefit period or benefit maximums,
- waiting period/elimination period,
- benefit amounts in different care environments,
- inflation protection,
- combination life insurance options,
- renewability, and
- tax deductibility of premiums

These variables, discussed below, and others, are very complex, and they change over time. It is imperative to shop around and discuss plan options with a specialist such as a financial planner who sells long-term care insurance policies.

It is advised that long-term care insurance policies should not consume more than 6-8% of your income. Those who are very wealthy might do better to save that 6-8% and invest it to cover any long-term care costs as they arise. Others simply cannot spare 6-8% of their income and may need to qualify for Medicaid if they ever need help with two or more ADLs previously mentioned. As with any insurance, such as flood insurance, you have to weigh the pros and cons of the various types of coverage and the various riders that are available.

Contact the American Association for Long-Term Care Insurance to find out more about these policies. www.aaltci.org.

Benefit Options

An LTC insurance policy may have a *benefit period* defining the number of coverage years that plan will pay out for your care. Such a policy may also contain *benefit maximums,* which are dollar amounts that can determine when coverage will end because you have used up the plan's maximum amount. Some plans offer coverage with no maximum, which means no matter how much is paid out for your care, the coverage will never end.

A *waiting period* is the amount of time you have to wait before the LTC plan will issue benefits. Most plans will begin paying benefits when the insured is unable to perform at least two activities of daily living (ADLs) for a period expected to last at least 90 days.

The *benefit amount* is how much money the plan will pay you daily or monthly (weekly benefit options are not very common anymore). Most policies allow you to choose a *daily or monthly benefit*. Daily benefit policies tend to be the least expensive and monthly the most expensive. The difference is flexibility, as explained below.

Example: You choose the *daily benefit option* and, let's say, it reimburses you $100 per day. Your home health aide costs $160 per day. You have a family member who can help you a couple of days a week and on the days you don't need a home health aide, the plan does not pay you the $100 per day. A *monthly benefit plan* might provide a total of $1000 per month for home or in-facility care. In this instance, you might have a home health aide for part of every day, or, you may need help only some days but not others. A monthly $1000 benefit will pay up to $1000 in benefits regardless of the number of separate days you use them. If your actual costs of care exceed the $1000 monthly, then you must make up the difference. If you had bought a $2000 per month benefit, then the numbers change accordingly.

With an *Indemnity Policy*, you get back all of your maximum benefit amount even if you don't spend that much on care. As an example, if you buy a $200 a day policy and your bill is $150 a day you still get $200 back. This is generally a more expensive type of policy than the Reimbursement model.

Additionally, many plans differentiate the amount of payout based on where you are receiving care. For example: a plan might pay $100 per day if you receive care in a facility, but only $50 per day if you receive care at home.

Inflation Rider

If you buy long-term care insurance and don't need it for years thereafter, you should not consider that you have wasted the premiums. The cost of health care could rise significantly in the interim. A very important option to consider when buying a plan is an "inflation rider." There are many types to choose from. For example, one policy might guarantee you a daily benefit increase of five percent per year based on the daily benefit you originally bought. Thus, your $100 per day benefit would increase to $105 in the second year in which you owned your policy. The daily benefit would then continue to rise each year by five percent of the original $100. After ten years, your daily benefit would be $145, or $4350 per month. If, however, you bought a policy that guaranteed you a daily benefit amount of five percent per year *compounded* each year, after ten years your benefit would be $163, or $4890 per month.

Purchasing a long-term care policy with a guaranteed compounded benefit amount will cost you more, but might very well be worth the extra expense. For younger people especially, buying a compounded inflation rider can help a great deal in offsetting the type of cost-of-care inflation seen historically. After twenty years, an original $100 daily benefit would have increased to $265.

LTC and Life Insurance Combinations

There are long-term care insurance policies that combine the long-term care coverage with *life insurance*. For example, you pay the company $100,000 for $400,000 worth of long-term care benefits. If you never use the long-term care benefits, your heirs will receive a "refund" of your original $100,000 premium plus interest. If you use only a portion of your long-term care benefits, your heirs will receive a partial refund. These policies are known as *combination policies*.

Premiums: Renewability

Long-term care insurance policies are generally *renewable*, but the premiums can be raised. They are not raised on the basis of your individual claims (like car insurance) but are based on external reasons. Long-term care insurance companies are not permitted to raise rates on individuals, but can only raise rates for an entire class of insured individuals. The combination life insurance and long-term care insurance policies require a large upfront "single premium." Policies that provide just long-term care insurance are much less expensive. According to a report by the American Association for Long-Term Care Insurance, more than forty percent of buyers under age 61 pay less than $1500 per year. Most buyers between age 61 and 75 pay $1500 or more.

If you do become sufficiently ill that your LTC insurance begins to pay benefits, further premium payments will be waived. If you recover and cease receiving benefits, your obligation to make premium payments resumes. Some people fail to pay their premiums because their mental condition has declined to the point where they are not paying their bills. Rather than lose coverage in that situation, those with LTC coverage can provide the insurance company with contact information for someone whom the insurance company can notify if his or her coverage is about to lapse for non-payment.

Premiums: Tax Deductibility

Some LTC insurance plans are tax-qualified, meaning that the payments you make in excess of a certain amount can be deducted for income tax purposes if you itemize your deductions. You can deduct your long-term care insurance premiums as part of your medical expenses once you exceed 10% of your adjusted gross income.

Attained age before the close of taxable year 2017:	Maximum deduction
40 or less	$410 (+5.1%)
More than 40 but not more than 50	$770
More than 50 but not more than 60	$1,530
More than 60 but not more than 70	$4090
More than 70	$5110 (+4.9%)

WHO'S GOING TO GET IT AFTER YOU'RE GONE?

Estate Planning Overview

In the "olden days," most people lived until their 60s at which time they got sick and died. They may have had family or friends to care for them and some medical advances to assist them, but, generally, when people got old and sick, they died soon thereafter. Their biggest concern was who would get their "stuff" after they were gone.

A Last Will and Testament (a.k.a. "a will"), was generally the only estate planning document needed and most people didn't even have that. In most states, the laws provided that family members ("heirs") would inherit when a person died "intestate," meaning he or she died without a will. For the most part, these heirs "at law" were the same people he or she would have named as beneficiaries in a will anyway.

Times have changed. Modern estate planning has to do with much more than who will get your stuff when you're gone. We are in an era of living longer and sometimes living for long periods of time when we are incapacitated either mentally or physically. Who will be your arms and legs if you become incapacitated? Who will make decisions for you if you cannot make them for yourself? Relatively recent changes in various laws now make it possible for you to plan ahead for what might happen if you were to become mentally or physically incapacitated. For most people, taking advantage of these planning opportunities is *much* more important than simply designating who will receive your assets after you die. Planning for possible incapacity allows you to decide ahead of time how, where and by whom you would like to be cared for in the worst case. Wills are good, of course, but you'll be gone by the time your will becomes effective. Planning for possible incapacity allows you to address issues that could affect the quality of your life while you're still living it.

If you do no estate planning at all, each state has its own rules about what happens if you become incapacitated. If you do become incapacitated, a court can generally appoint a Guardian of your person and a Conservator of your assets. Guardians not infrequently simply admit their wards to nursing homes even if the ward has enough money for home care; the conservator uses the ward's money to pay the nursing home until the ward dies or his or her money runs out. Then the conservator will apply for Medicaid if need be.

Given the power a court appointee can have over your care or the management of your money/estate, it is advisable to have legal documents prepared while you are healthy wherein you choose in advance whom you prefer to act on your behalf if you cannot manage your own affairs. This is done by executing legal documents such as financial and healthcare powers of attorney, a living will and other advance medical directives. You can plan for the distribution of your assets upon your death using a will or a trust. If you do not make arrangements for how your matters should be handled both during your lifetime and after your death, you and/or your assets will be handled in accordance with the particular law in your state.

Planning allows you to maximize your own comfort, using your own assets, for as long as possible. Depending on how much money you have, you can plan to be cared for in your own home with companions to take you on outings or assure that you have your favorite foods. If you simply cannot afford to be cared for at home, you can at least assure that your care in an institution is monitored to guard against abuse or neglect - and that someone brings you your weekly box of chocolates. Planning for possible incapacity can assure that you always have visitors, care monitors and little luxuries that make your life more pleasant.

And if you never become incapacitated, if you never need someone to make medical, financial or care decisions on your behalf, would you have "wasted" the money and effort to do the planning? Have you wasted all of the fire insurance premiums you've paid for your home? There are no guarantees except that if you do become incapacitated without such planning, you will have forfeited the opportunity to enhance your own quality of life during your last days. This is the type of planning that you hope you will never need. But if you do need it, you **really** need it. A good source for all types of estate planning and elder law questions is www.elderlawanswers.com.

Last Will and Testament

A *will* is a "last will and testament" which operates only after death. It is a document that you sign with the necessary legally-required witnesses that directs how you would like your assets to be distributed after your death. You use a will to name a person to be an "executor" or personal representative to distribute your estate according to your directions.

You can make as many wills as you like, but every time you make a new one you revoke your prior will. There can only ever be *one* valid will at a time. Except for a few rare exceptions, the will presented to the court after your death must be an original will, not a copy of a will. The absence of an original can create a legal presumption that it was revoked or destroyed on purpose. Make sure your loved ones know where to find your will. A safe deposit box is not a good place to keep it. The legal authority to open the box is usually granted by the terms of your will itself. Thus, the key, that is the will itself, is in the box.

If you die "intestate" (with no will or trust with designated beneficiaries of your assets), each state has a process by which a court oversees the distribution of your property to your creditors and to a set list of heirs. The individual who actually pays your debts and distributes your remaining assets is known as an administrator or personal representative. Under a will, the personal representative is usually called an "executor."

An estate is everything a person controls, owns alone, or sometimes jointly, at the time of his or her death. Property which might pass under your will is described as being "tangible personal property," "intangible personal property" or "real property." Tangible personal property is something you can touch and move around, such as art, jewelry, pots and pans, your car, the grandfather clock. Intangible personal property is property whose value is not something you can touch, but is represented usually by paper documents. Cash, bank accounts, investment accounts, retirement programs, stocks and bonds are examples of intangible personal property. Real property is real estate such as land, your home, your beach condo. Tangible and intangible personal property are certainly "real," but for purposes of your estate, only real estate is referred to as "real property."

A will does not need to name every item of tangible personal property of importance to you and what should become of it when you pass away. In most (or all) jurisdictions the will can mention a separate list, which you can change or add to whenever you want, that lists all those specific little items such as jewelry and the good china and directs what your executor should do with them. The list is then "incorporated by reference" into your will and thereby becomes an actual part of your will. Where use of this procedure is permitted, such a list allows you to add items you obtain after you create your will, change the identified recipients, or take items off of the list you no longer have without having to re-execute a whole new will every time. Thus, you can change your mind about who gets the diamond bracelet without having to go back to a lawyer to do a new will.

If your will directs your executor generally to divide tangible items among your heirs, be sure to specify how the executor should do it. Avoid family arguments regarding items you have not included on your specific list by planning ahead. For example, you could direct that your beneficiaries draw names from a hat to determine who gets first choice (regardless of monetary or sentimental value), and how they should take turns naming their next first choice among your possessions. All efforts should be made to avoid the problem of more than one person claiming: "mom promised I could have that after she died." Some families experience permanent alienation due to arguments over who gets which item of tangible personal property. It is a problem that is important and easy to avoid.

Probate

After you die, a court will "probate" your will. Probate is a court-supervised process by which your estate is administered. The word "probate" is of Latin derivation meaning "to prove"; therefore, probate is where it is proved under law that your will is authentic and therefore governs how you wish your estate to be distributed. For a fee charged to your estate assets, the court will oversee the process by which your debts are paid and your wishes as stated in your will are actually carried out by the executor you chose.

Note: it is important for parents of young children to consider a will to designate a guardian for their minor children.

Additionally, a will can provide that certain assets should be held in "trust" for specific beneficiaries, such as minor or disabled children. Such trusts created by a will are called testamentary trusts; they are also often used for tax planning. Wills with trusts must be very carefully drafted for those who have complicated financial situations such as second marriages and stepchildren. Either the law or provisions of the trust itself may also require the trustee to provide ongoing reports and continuing fees to the court. Such reporting requirements can usually be waived, if desired, by explicit provisions in the will itself.

There is also a type of will referred to as a *Pour Over Will*. It is used in conjunction with a Revocable Living Trust (RLT) (see RLT discussion below). Instead of directing the distribution of your property to particular people, it "pours" all of your assets into your RLT. Assets not already titled in the name of your trust would be placed into the trust by the named executor. Then the instructions in the trust become applicable as to who will receive what assets and whether new trusts for some beneficiaries will be created, and so forth.

To begin the probate process, someone (family, friend, or executor) takes the original will to the court in the locality where the person died and "files for probate." The named executor then "qualifies" as such before the court. If that person is unavailable (perhaps deceased), the court will use state statutes to determine whom to appoint as a suitable alternate. The alternate then becomes the personal representative. Alternate personal representatives are sometimes referred to as administrators. These terms can also be used when someone dies *intestate* (with no will).

After being approved by the court, the executor then has legal authority to locate and gather estate assets, pay creditors and court fees, file and pay estate and income taxes, distribute the remaining assets to the designated recipient(s), or, if none are still living, to whomever the will designates as alternate beneficiaries. In the absence of a provision in the will itself, the property in question will be distributed as state statute directs. One option is to name a charity as the "fall back" beneficiary in case all of your named beneficiaries are deceased.

The executor is required to provide an accounting to the court of all the estate assets, payments, and distributions. Some states have separate probate courts for this purpose. In other areas, the court appoints someone with relevant experience to oversee the administration of the estate. In Virginia, for example, the courts of each county appoint a Commissioner of Accounts in their locality. For their work, executors receive either an amount set forth in the will or "reasonable compensation" as a fee for their services. The fee can range from 1% to 5% of the estate assets, and the probate process usually takes at least six months and sometimes considerably longer, even years.

Estate beneficiaries who do not want to inherit anything must disclaim their inheritance within nine months of the death and cannot take any benefit from the disclaimed assets before disclaiming. They cannot decide who will get their share. It goes back into the estate "pot" and passes as if the disclaimant died before the testator, (the person who died with a will.) Why would someone do this? One frequent reason involves fairly sophisticated estate tax issues. A well-to-do parent will often disclaim assets that then automatically go to his or her child.

Even if you have executed a will that says it is disposing of *all* of your assets, some assets might pass directly to their new owners without having to go through the probate process. Examples include property titled with another person as "joint tenants with right of survivorship," life insurance proceeds, investment and retirement accounts that name a beneficiary, and bank accounts that are titled "pay on death" (POD) which name a person who automatically receives the money in the account when you die. For investment accounts, the equivalent to a POD designation is a TOD designation – "transfer on death." The named beneficiary needs to have a death certificate to claim such property or assets.

As a matter of practice, executors should have enough death certificates for each individual or account which might need one. Death certificates are usually easy to obtain from funeral homes shortly after a decedent's death. If the death certificates are not obtained at that time, those who need one must go through whatever process their state might require for obtaining certified copies of public records.

Most married couples in non-community property states own their houses as "tenants by the entirety" which is a special form of joint ownership just for married couples. During the lifetimes of both spouses, this form of ownership protects the family home in the event that a creditor of one spouse might try to seize it to repay a debt of that one spouse. Upon the death of one spouse, the surviving spouse will automatically own the whole house without having to take any legal steps. The house becomes the sole property of the surviving spouse "by operation of law." No new deed is required. If the surviving spouse decides to sell the house, the title searcher will find both the earlier "tenants by the entirety" deed and the death certificate of the deceased tenant by the entirety. Property held as tenants by the entirety will usually not be subject to creditors as would the half of the house owned by non-married people who may own property simply as "joint tenants" or "tenants in common." These terms and their legal effect vary from state to state.

To determine what will provisions would be best for you and your beneficiaries, you should consult with an elder law/estate planning attorney. See www.naela.org.

Testamentary Capacity

Mom died at 81 leaving an estate of about $600,000, including her home located in a close-in Washington DC suburb. She had two children. Her son, a well-to-do banker, earns a very good living and resides in an affluent suburb outside of New York City. Mom's daughter was employed by a non-profit world food aid program in Washington. She could have earned much more in the private sector but she loved her job and had the satisfaction of helping others.

Mom's will left two-thirds of her estate to her daughter and one-third to her son.

Son was upset. He thought he should have received half of mom's estate. Like many adult children, he felt that parents "should" leave their estates to their children in equal shares. Actually, most parents do that. But many do not. When family relations are not secure, unequal testamentary distribution will often cause the "short-changed" child to question whether mom really knew what she was doing when she signed the will; that is, did mom have testamentary capacity? Hard on the heels of the testamentary capacity issue is the question of whether mom was subjected to undue influence by her daughter.

So, what is testamentary capacity? And what is undue influence?

First, testamentary capacity requires the testator to know what she's doing at the time she's doing it – that is, making a will to dispose of her property after she dies. She has to know the general nature and extent of her assets, the natural objects of her bounty (in this case, her two children) and how she wishes to have her assets distributed after her death. What many disappointed family members often forget is that the assets belong to mom. There is no such thing as "my inheritance" until someone has died and left you something. Mom's estate does not belong to those who expect to inherit it. How and to whom she leaves her estate is up to mom. If she chooses to disinherit both children and give all of her worldly possessions to a homeless shelter, that decision is hers to make.

It's when unequal distributions are made to adult children, or when they are made to someone the family thinks was taking advantage of mom, that these issues most frequently arise. Mom's health had been steadily declining over several years leading up to the time of the execution of her will. She lived for another two years, ultimately needing a 24/7 home health aide in order to remain in her home.

When mom's health began to decline and she could no longer drive, daughter visited every week-end to take mom shopping for groceries, unload them and put them away and do other errands such as picking up prescriptions and filling mom's pill boxes for the week. Daughter called mom every morning to make sure she had taken her morning pills. She called every evening to see how her day had been and to remind her to take her nighttime pills. By calling mom twice a day, daughter could confirm that mom was ok so far. For in-between hours, daughter obtained a two-way communication life-link device, which connected to a service which would assist immediately if mom pushed the button.

As mom's health declined, daughter arranged for a home health aide to come in for several hours in the morning and in the late afternoon. The aide assisted mom with bathing, prepared breakfast and left lunch in the refrigerator. The late afternoon aide gave mom dinner, cleaned up and settled mom for the evening in her nightgown and robe. Daughter stopped by often to make sure all was well. Mom and daughter became very close. With daughter's assistance, both in terms of her personal visits and contacts and in her management of mom's care, mom lived securely in her own home until her death.

Son was very busy with his career and family in New York. He called mom every few months to check in and he sent lovely flowers for Christmas, Mother's Day and mom's birthday. He periodically called his sister to inquire about mom but he never offered any assistance. Fortunately, mom had a good income from her late husband's annuity and Social Security. She had been dipping into her savings nest egg to pay for the home health aides, but she was basically secure.

When mom asked daughter to set up an appointment with a lawyer so she could make a new will, daughter did so and took mom to the appointment. Mom met privately with the attorney. She loved both of her children. For several reasons, however, including her wish to reward her daughter's selfless care as well as recognizing her daughter's modest financial position, mom thought the fairest distribution of her estate would be to give her daughter two-thirds and her son one-third of her assets. She actually considered leaving all of it to her daughter since her son was already very well-to-do. She thought that her son would approve of his mother's rationale for financially favoring her daughter. When she asked the attorney if he thought this distribution would be fair under the circumstances, the attorney reminded her that it was her money and she could do whatever she wanted to do with it.

However, this attorney was an elder law attorney and he had seen many family problems emerge from such unequal distributions, especially when the favored child had been the elder's primary caregiver. He encouraged mom to do two things: 1. Consent to an evaluation of her mental condition by a physician or a professional geriatric care manager (GCM), and 2. Sign an additional "dear family" letter explaining her decision and emphasizing that the unequal distribution in no way reflected unequal love for her children. She described her reasoning in her own words; the attorney's paralegal typed it up. When she executed the will, the attorney made sure that she had a chance to chat with the witnesses and that, without going into the details of her will, she exhibited both to him and to the witnesses that she possessed testamentary capacity.

Undue Influence

Unequal distributions and distributions to individuals who are not the "natural objects of the testator's bounty" also generate allegations that the favored beneficiary exercised "undue influence" over the testator. An undue influence claim acknowledges that the testator had testamentary capacity, but alleges that he or she had been subject to the "undue influence" of the favored beneficiary.

The son described above could have alleged that his sister used her position of trust to influence her mother to favor daughter in her will.

To prove undue influence, the claimant must argue that the favored beneficiary occupied a position of special trust and was, therefore, in a position to influence the testator's will. Positions of trust include not just adult children or other relatives who provide care, but automatically include attorneys-in-fact, or agents, serving under a durable power of attorney, trustees and other fiduciaries. (See later discussion of attorneys-in-fact and trustees.)

The burden of proving an allegation of undue influence is on the person claiming it, but that burden can shift if the benefited person occupied a fiduciary position. Each case will be determined on its individual merit. On the facts in the example above, wherein sister gets two-thirds of mom's estate, an allegation of undue influence would likely fail if for no other reason than the fact that daughter provided such loving care over a substantial period of time. Without daughter's care and care management, mom would have lived her last days in a nursing home. If mom's signed statement explaining her reasoning, the physician's or geriatric care manager's (GCM; see later discussion) evaluation, and the testimony of the witnesses are added to the mix, the allegation would most likely not be pursued at all.

Lucid Interval

What if mom had been diagnosed with Alzheimer's Disease at the time of her death? And what if the disease had been slowly progressing over a number of years? Can a person with a dementing illness possess testamentary capacity? The answer is yes. In the above case, testamentary capacity was clearly present. But what if mom was seriously deteriorating mentally at the time she signed her will? The answer will come down to the particular facts and circumstances of the case. Even a very ill person can have a "lucid interval" during which he possesses the elements of testamentary capacity. There have been numerous cases in which an individual has been adjudicated by a court as needing a conservator to manage his/her financial affairs, but who still can be considered to possess testamentary capacity. Whether or not the testator possessed testamentary capacity during a lucid interval is a question of fact. The court will consider evidence such as that described above as to whether the necessary capacity was present at the time the will was executed.

In one famous very early case, a woman had been found by a court to be a "lunatic" and was committed to a "lunatic asylum" (that's how long ago the case was decided). She owned substantial assets. During her confinement, the natural objects of her bounty never visited her, whereas some cousins came on a regular basis, bringing her gifts and treats. Eventually she called for a lawyer and executed a will naming these cousins as her beneficiaries. The disinherited natural objects of her bounty attacked the will, claiming that as an adjudicated "lunatic" she, by definition, lacked testamentary capacity. They lost. The court held that a finding that an individual is unable to manage his or her affairs has value as evidence in a testamentary capacity challenge, but it does not settle the issue. Whether the individual possessed testamentary capacity during a lucid interval was a question of fact. It would be decided by the jury (or judge, as the case may be), after considering all the facts and circumstances including, especially, the testimony of the witnesses to the will.

Estate and Inheritance Taxes

Estate Taxes, both federal and state (in some states), are taxes your estate must pay based on the value of your assets, including those that can pass outside the probate process, such as joint accounts, IRAs and life insurance policies which have designated beneficiaries. If the probate estate is not sufficient to pay taxes, the executor, depending on applicable law, can force the non-probate beneficiaries to contribute. Some, but not all, states have an estate tax. For example, Virginia has no state estate tax. Washington D.C. does. Regarding Federal Estate Tax rates: in 2017, if your estate is worth more than $5.49 million, each dollar over $5.49 million will be taxed at 40%. The 40% rate is expected to remain the same, however, the dollar amount limit will rise based on inflation. For instance, the limit was $5 million even in 2013 and has been creeping upward.

Inheritance Taxes differ from estate taxes. Some, but not all, states impose inheritance taxes. There is no federal inheritance tax. Inheritance taxes are computed based on the share of particular beneficiaries' inheritances. The inheritance tax due on property left to an immediate family member will generally be lower than that levied on the same amount of assets distributed to the neighbor down the street. Generally speaking, in states that have inheritance taxes, close relatives are taxed at low rates such as 1%; unrelated beneficiaries, such as neighbors, can be taxed at higher rates such as 10%.

Any detailed discussion of estate, inheritance or gift tax issues, at either the federal or state levels, is simply too complex for this book. If you are well-to-do, you should consult with an estate planning or elder law attorney.

FINANCIAL POWER OF ATTORNEY
(Commonly Referred to as POA)

POA Overview

A power of attorney is a document by which a "principal" (the person who signs the document) gives another person, (the "attorney-in-fact" or "agent,") authority to act on behalf of the principal. Typically, durable powers of attorney authorize the agent to carry out financial tasks such as signing the principal's checks, dealing with his assets, investing his money and generally handling his financial affairs.

It is important to note that a POA is not legally obligated to take action with the tasks you appoint to them, unlike a Trustee, who must take action to follow your instructions in a Trust, as long as they are the acting Trustee. Example: a POA is allowed to pay your bills, but it doesn't mean they have to. If a Trustee is directed to pay your bills, they must pay your bills.

Although it is the document itself which is the "power of attorney," referring to the attorney-in-fact or agent as "the POA" has come into popular usage. Thus, both usages will be used in these discussions. For example, Mary Smith, daughter and POA of her mom, Jane Smith, might sign checks as "Mary Smith, POA" rather than the more formal "Mary Smith, Attorney-in-Fact for Jane Smith," or "Jane Smith by Mary Smith, Attorney-in-Fact."

Prior to the late 1980s when POAs began to be commonly used, the only avenue open to allow for the management of the business affairs of an incapacitated person was a court proceeding to obtain appointment of a guardian and/or conservator. Thus, DPOAs are known as "guardianship avoidance devices."

The word "durable" means that the POA will remain valid even if the principal becomes incapacitated. Indeed, authorizing someone else to handle your affairs in the event of your incapacity has become one of the most important estate planning-for-life actions you can take. Your bills and other financial responsibilities can be carried out by your POA, thus avoiding any need for a court to order a conservator for your affairs. If and when you recover capacity, you just go back to handling things yourself.

Unlike a will, you can execute multiple originals of a power of attorney document. Having at least two originals of the power of attorney document can be handy. For example, if your POA is authorized to sell your residence, and does so, an original of the POA document must be recorded with the deed. Title searchers look for language in the POA document which specifically authorizes the sale of the particular real estate in question. Simply saying "my agent can sell any of my property" will often not be considered adequate and can delay or even block the sale. If you have only one original of the document, it may be temporarily unavailable after being recorded. While awaiting proof of recordation, your POA might need to open an account in your name and the bank might want to see an original document.

As is true of other estate planning documents, there is no such thing as "one size fits all" when it comes to POAs. Your specific property, your specific family situation and your specific goals must be taken in account by the drafter of the document.

Uniform Power of Attorney Act (UPOAA)

Almost every state has adopted a version of the *Uniform Power of Attorney Act (UPOAA)* which substantially clarifies and standardizes laws related to Durable Powers of Attorney.

For example, under the UPOAA, all powers of attorney are presumed to be durable unless otherwise stated in the document. This is a reversal of common law.

The UPOAA also provides protection for third parties who in good faith rely on a purportedly properly executed power of attorney, and it provides sanctions against third parties if they unreasonably refuse to honor POA documents.

The UPOAA identifies certain very sensitive powers, such as the gift-giving powers described above, that must be specifically granted in the language of the document; in addition to expansive powers to make gifts of the principal's assets, such powers might also include powers to transfer assets, change beneficiary designations on the principal's insurance and retirement programs, or even to create or amend a trust.

Gift-Giving Power

Can your POA give away your money? Can he pay himself for his services as POA? Some powers are so sensitive that they cannot be exercised unless they are specifically spelled out in the document. The most common example of this involves gift-giving. Do you want your POA to continue to give your children $1,000 on their birthdays? If so, spell out the power, who the recipients can be, and what dollar limit applies to gifts. What if one of your children is the person serving as your POA? Can he make one of those gifts to himself? Agents are generally prohibited from making gifts to themselves. Doing so would constitute self-dealing. So, if your child-POA is to be a permissible recipient, the POA document must expressly say so.

Spouses in long-term stable marriages usually appoint each other to serve as their POAs. In the discussion on Medicaid planning for married couples, you will see that it is necessary for the "well" spouse to transfer all assets of the "ill" spouse to herself. Assuming the ill spouse is legally incapacitated at the time Medicaid might be needed, the well spouse must have a POA authorizing her (or him, as the case may be) to transfer *all* of the ill spouse's assets into her own name. In this case, the POA spouse could give herself *all* of her spouse's assets. Indeed, doing so is essential to the process of spousal Medicaid planning.

Without express authorization, the well spouse, acting as her spouse's POA, cannot legally make those transfers, thus precluding Medicaid eligibility. In a worst case, that reality will force both spouses into the traumatic, costly and not always successful process of obtaining a court-ordered guardianship/conservatorship which allows Medicaid planning. Reciprocal spousal gift-giving powers must be included in the POA expressly. This works fine for the 50-year happily married couple. It could be a disaster for someone whose spouse might be tempted to abscond with all of the marital property.

POA Compensation

Generally, POAs are friends or family members and are not paid for their services. However, to reduce the burden on family or friends, or to provide an incentive to the POA to continue serving, you may wish to provide for payment for the POA's services. If you choose to pay someone, the terms for the payment must be stated within the body of the document. Otherwise the rules against "self-dealing" would apply and any payment *by* the POA *to* the POA would be prohibited. These rules apply to family members and friends as well as professionals who serve as POAs.

In practice, when the principal's incapacity is expected to be lengthy or permanent, POAs might find it helpful to order checks in both the account owner's name and their name so they can just sign their name and then write "POA," thus avoiding the more lengthy version "Jane Smith by Mary Smith, Attorney-in-Fact."

Durability

Today, virtually all financial POA documents are *durable*. Before the enactment of Durable POA laws, powers of attorney were automatically invalidated if the principal became incapacitated. They weren't "durable," or strong enough, to survive the principal's incapacity. All powers of attorney, durable or otherwise, become invalid upon the death of the principal. As a POA, you are supposed to act as if you were "standing in the shoes" of the person who appointed you, and conducting their business just as they would have themselves, and not how you yourself would manage things. You can't act in another person's shoes so to speak when they are no longer alive.

Modern POAs are usually effective immediately upon execution, even though the intention is that they would be used only in the event of the principal's incapacity. Some POAs are "springing"; they "spring" into effectiveness upon the incapacity of the principal. At first glance this seems to be a good idea. The problem is: How does the POA prove to the banker that the principal is incapacitated? Going back to conservatorship court for a finding of incapacity defeats the purpose of the durable POA.

Durable POAs can also be *Limited* or *Special*. Such POA documents usually grant a narrow power such as the legal authority to act for a sole purpose. A good example is granting a limited, or special, power of attorney for another person to sign closing documents at settlement on the sale of real property.

The agent (person being granted the power of attorney AKA POA) does not have to be present to sign the document at the time it is executed by the principal. Nevertheless, it is a good idea to have a "specimen signature" of the POA notarized at the same time the principal's signature is notarized. Different states have different witness and notary requirements.

The individual appointed to serve as Power of Attorney has a legal fiduciary duty to act on your behalf and can be held liable in court for violating that obligation. Consequently, it is very important to choose someone you trust; you should also name a back-up or successor POA in the document in case something happens to your first choice.

For those who are fortunate enough to have in their lives people whom they trust absolutely, executing a POA can be one of the most valuable things they can do for themselves.

NOTE: Many investment companies prefer to have their own Power of Attorney Documents signed. Even though the POA you execute in an attorney's office will include the power to handle investments if you so choose, investment companies may not make using those documents easy. Play it on the safe side. If you have a firm or company that handles investments for you, contact them as soon as you execute a POA and ask them if they have their own forms to "parallel" the powers you are granting through your general POA. It does sound redundant, but it will make things a lot easier in the end.

DO-IT-YOURSELF ESTATE PLANNING?

Will Examples

There are many websites available which offer templates for wills, trusts, powers of attorney and Advance Medical Directives; bookstores also sell such forms. Each state has different requirements about what makes a document legally binding. A website can provide forms which are in fact actually "compliant" with the laws of the state in question. But do the forms adequately address your particular situation? If you've been married to your only spouse for fifty years and have responsible adult children who are not married to someone you can't stand, forms might work. Being compliant with state law, however, doesn't necessarily mean that a document you execute will actually produce the desired results under the law of your particular state.

Example: John and Mary Taylor were married for fifty years. John married Mary when she was a young widow with two toddlers. Two other children came along in due course. John and Mary raised the children to be responsible adults. They were a close family. Mary dies. John obtains a pre-printed Last Will and Testament form. In the place where he is to write how he wants his estate to be distributed, he says "I leave everything I own to my children in equal shares."

Who will get his assets? In the context of wills, the simple word "children" can have different meanings in different jurisdictions. John intends for each of his four children to have a share of his estate. To him, to Mary and to the children themselves, the children were his and Mary's children, and they are all each other's siblings. Period. But John never formally adopted the two older children. Result: John's entire estate will go to the two younger children; nothing will go to the two older children. In John's jurisdiction, stepchildren do not count as "children" despite a lifetime of living as members of a family with four children.

Example: Robert and Joan Williams have been married for fifty years. They have two children. Joan develops Alzheimer's Disease and is now a Medicaid recipient residing in a long-term care nursing home. Robert still owns the family home and the assets he was permitted to retain when Joan qualified for Medicaid. His old will left everything to Joan. He knows that leaving assets to Joan would disqualify her from continued receipt of Medicaid benefits. Robert downloads a state-compliant will from a website. In the dispositive section he says "I leave everything to my two children in equal shares." What will the two children actually get?

Unbeknownst to Robert, his state has a law that allows a disinherited spouse to elect to take one-half of the decedent spouse's estate, regardless of what the will says. But Joan is in a nursing home; she is not capable of "electing" anything. <u>However, what she can't do for herself, Medicaid will be happy to do for her.</u> A spouse who does not claim his or her elective share of a decedent spouse's estate will be considered by Medicaid to have made a gift of that share – in this case, a gift to the two children. Such a gift would disqualify Joan from continued eligibility for Medicaid. Medicaid would consider her failure to claim her share of her late husband's estate to be a disqualifying transfer of assets for less than fair market value to her two children. Medicaid can go to court and claim Joan's elective share for her. Joan will then have too much money for Medicaid eligibility; her conservator will spend her share of Robert's estate on private pay for her nursing home care. If and when that money runs out, Joan will again be qualified for Medicaid.

But what if there's still money left when Joan dies. Will that go to her two children? Probably not. Medicaid has a right of "estate recovery," meaning that they can assert a claim for reimbursement against Joan's estate for the Medicaid-covered care she received before Robert died.

Was there anything Robert could have done to assure that his children would actually receive more than half of his estate? If Robert had consulted with an elder law attorney before executing a new will, he could have left a special needs trust (SNT, see later discussion) for the benefit of Joan for the remainder of her life, and upon her death, the trust share would go to his children as an addition to the one-half of Robert's estate they've already received. What was in the trust is not part of Joan's "estate." Remaining assets belong to the SNT. Rules regarding such special needs trusts, if permitted in Robert's jurisdiction, can be quite technical. But if Robert had known about that option, which provides for Joan's special needs to be met while also assuring a larger inheritance for his children, he would likely have chosen it.

The pre-printed form Robert used may have been "compliant" with state law, but it failed to produce the result that Robert intended.

Then there's the straightforward case of Stanley and Alice. Married for fifty years, they have reciprocal "I love you" wills in which they each leave everything to each other, if he or she is the surviving spouse, and if neither spouse survives, then the estate goes to the children in equal shares. They downloaded their will forms from the internet. These wills worked just fine. But in most jurisdictions, the result would have been the same if Stanley and Alice had no wills at all. They could have saved their efforts: under the law of intestate (no will) succession in their example state, the law provides that the estate of a decedent will pass to his or her surviving spouse, and if there is no surviving spouse, then to the children.

People in second marriages with children from the first, or second, or both marriages should be aware that a "simple" will can have unforeseen and unintended consequences. How about Samuel? He has two children from his first marriage. He left his first wife to marry his present wife. In his will, he wants to provide for the support of his present wife for her lifetime, and if anything is left over, he wants it to go to his adult children. How will he accomplish this? Assuming he leaves a trust for the benefit of his wife, how should it be structured? He wants to avoid having his wife/widow be subject to complaints by his children that she's spending too much money. What if she remarries? This situation is full of landmines and definitely requires the advice of an experienced estate planning or elder law attorney.

People who wish to prepare their own wills should think about their situations very carefully. They should "walk through" in their minds how they actually wish to distribute their estates. They should imagine the "what if" possibilities. Then they should consider whether the do-it-yourself will really does "do it."

Durable Power of Attorney Examples

Mentioned above was Joan Williams, wife of Robert. Robert had been able to retain the family home, buy a good new car, install a new furnace and keep about $120,900 in liquid assets, (see section on Medicaid for married couples for the origin of that dollar amount), while Joan qualified for long-term care Medicaid. Joan had been the joint owner of the home and the bank account and she had a $15,000 savings account which held her portion of an inheritance she received from another family member. The home was exempt under Medicaid law, but her interest in the joint account and her savings account would disqualify her for as long as those accounts still had her name on them. She would not qualify for nursing home Medicaid until she had less than $2000. (See later discussion of Medicaid for Married Couples.)

So how was Robert able to become the sole owner of the family home and transfer to himself Joan's interest in the joint account and her ownership of her $15,000 savings account? Robert and Joan had visited an elder law attorney because they were concerned about what would happen if one of them were later diagnosed with Alzheimer's Disease or some other incapacitating illness. They told their attorney that they wanted her to represent both of them and they waived attorney-client privilege as to each other. Review of the Williams' financial situation showed that if one of the spouses required nursing home care, they would either need to qualify for Medicaid or go bankrupt.

The attorney told Robert and Joan that they could execute durable powers of attorney that would allow either of them to take all of the assets of the other if one of them needed to qualify for Medicaid. Asset transfers between spouses are exempt for Medicaid purposes. The power of an attorney-in-fact to give himself or herself all of the assets of the principal is not a provision to be found in pre-printed form POA documents. An attorney-in-fact who converts all of the Principal's assets to himself is, absent express authority in the document, engaging in prohibited self-dealing. Such transfers can be voided. Yet it was that very power that might be needed by Robert and Joan. Without it, Robert would have had no choice but to endure the expense, trauma and delay of obtaining a guardianship/conservatorship over Joan and seek the court's approval of an order permitting him to take all of Joan's assets. There was a time when some courts would refuse to issue such orders claiming that facilitating eligibility for a welfare program was against public policy. These days, courts generally recognize that the Medicaid rules to prevent the impoverishment of a community spouse were intentionally enacted by the Congress for that very purpose.

What if the exempt house had been left jointly titled in Robert's and Joan's names? Joan could still have qualified for Medicaid because her ownership interest in the house is an exempt asset. But what if Robert later decides to sell the house, using power of attorney forms signed by Joan and Robert which they bought at a bookstore? Most POA forms contain some general powers to the effect that the POA authorizes the POA-agent to do and perform every act that the Principal can do. The POA is authorized to sign deeds, purchase, acquire, buy, sell, convey, mortgage, pledge, lease or otherwise transfer any and all property, real and personal. Within this shopping list of powers, will Robert have authority sufficient to persuade a lender or a title company that he has Joan's authority to sell *this particular* house?

There may be some jurisdictions in which a "general powers" clause such as that described above might be considered sufficient to authorize the POA to sell the house. The more typical situation is that a POA must explicitly identify each piece of real property subject to the power of sale in the document; it must be identified either by its address or by its legal description. Without that explicit power to sell that particular house, the one belonging to Robert and Joan, Robert will have to seek a court order allowing him to (1) transfer Joan's interest to him and then (2) sell the house as his sole property. If he had sold the house under authority of a sufficiently explicit POA or under a court order allowing him to sell Joan's interest, Joan's portion of the sales proceeds would knock her off of Medicaid. It was essential that Robert's and Joan's power of attorney documents authorize the "well" spouse to transfer to himself all assets of the "ill" spouse. As noted, if Robert simply used the POA Joan signed to sell the house which was still titled in both of their names, one-half of the proceeds of such a sale would belong to Joan, putting her over her asset limit for Medicaid purposes.

HOW TRUSTS CAN BENEFIT YOU WHILE YOU'RE STILL AROUND

Revocable Living Trust (RLT) Overview

A Revocable Living Trust (RLT) is established by a grantor, also called a settler or trustor, during his or her lifetime. A typical RLT appoints the grantor himself or herself as both initial trustee and sole lifetime beneficiary. Although probate avoidance is often cited as a principal reason for choosing a trust-based estate plan over that which relies primarily on a will, an RLT can contain not just the individual's "after death" wishes, but also legally binding instructions for how his or her money and care should be handled in the event of incapacity.

A trust with the word "living" in it simply means the trust becomes effective during the grantor's lifetime.

This type of planning is especially valuable for those who may have concerns about adult children or other heirs who would like to "save more of their inheritance" by spending *less*, rather than more, of an incapacitated grantor's *own* assets on keeping him or her comfortable and well cared for. Powers of Attorney (POAs) can authorize the POA to spend whatever is needed to care for the principal at home. But a POA is not legally required to carry out such wishes. The POA is mere authority to act, not a requirement. A trustee, on the other hand, is under a legal duty to follow the instructions in the trust.

Fully funded trusts are also used as substitutes for wills. To "fund" an RLT, the grantor would change the name on his or her property, such as bank accounts and title to the residence, from the name of the grantor in his or her individual capacity to the name of the grantor in his or her capacity as trustee of his or her own trust.

For example, a bank account titled in the name of Mary Jones would be retitled by simply going to the bank and changing the account name to Mary Jones, Trustee of the Mary Jones trust dated 1/1/2013. Mary Jones' own social security number continues as the tax identification number for the account. A home can be retitled by recording a new deed changing ownership from Mary Jones in her individual capacity to Mary Jones, Trustee, and so forth. The deed should make clear that any successor trustee to Mary has the same trust powers and authority to deal with that real property as Mary herself had before her death or incapacity.

You can think of your RLT as an empty box. As you retitle your assets into your own name as trustee of your own trust, you are "putting" those assets into the box. Of course, you can also remove anything from the "box" whenever you wish. It's still your property. All assets in the "box" will be managed in accordance with the instructions you put in the trust document. If you become incapacitated, your POA can provide that assets not yet retitled, should be retitled into your name (or that of a successor you appoint) as trustee, thereby subjecting those assets to the instructions in the trust.

If assets remain "outside the box" at your death, they would be put into the box by your **Pour Over Will** - that is, a will which simply says something to the effect that "anything I own in my own name when I die should be distributed to my trust." Then the "will-type" language of your trust takes over. Please note, the title of the document that effectively acts as the will to pour your assets over into your trust will simply be called "Last Will and Testament" or some variation, and won't say "Pour Over" on it.

Sometimes people create trusts on paper (they build an empty box) and never bother to "fund" the trust at all by re-titling accounts and other assets. As noted, their wishes for both lifetime care and after-death distribution, as expressed in their trust, can still be effective. Not funding a trust, however, can cause unnecessary probate fees and delays. If you have a trust, take the time to fund it. Your attorney can help you do it.

Advantages of a Revocable Living Trust

One advantage of establishing a funded RLT is that its contents remain private, unlike a will filed at a courthouse for anyone to read. This has traditionally made trusts a popular estate planning choice among people who value personal privacy.

Another advantage of a funded RLT applies to people who own houses, land or other real property in a different state. If that property is held as a trust asset, whoever is trustee (before or after the grantor's death) can deal with the property. If, however, an individual dies owning out-of-state property in his or her individual name, the executor of the probate estate will have to hire an attorney in that other state to conduct an "ancillary probate" of that property. This can be costly and result in unnecessary delays.

The most frequently cited advantage of an RLT is probate avoidance. If all of your assets are held in your name as trustee of your own trust, then there are no assets in your individual name to pass through probate. In reality, however, many people execute RLTs without ever "funding" their trusts, so everything has to go through probate anyway. Decedent's estates have to be administered one way or the other. Choosing an RLT solely for the purpose of avoiding probate may not be worth the extra expense and effort unless there is some other motivating reason to have an RLT.

At the time the trust is created, the trust grantor/settlor/trustor (different names for the same person) appoints a trustee (usually himself or herself) who holds the key to the lock on the box that holds trust assets. Most people appoint themselves to be the trustee for as long as they are alive and mentally competent (so they are both the grantor and trustee). They then appoint in their trust a successor trustee, or sometimes joint successor trustees, to act as trustee if he or she, the grantor and original trustee, cannot act due to death or incapacity.

Trustees who succeed the original grantor-trustee upon that person's death or incapacity receive fees for their work. This fee is often a small percentage of the trust assets. Some people appoint family members as successor trustees. Others appoint an institution or paid professional to be a trustee, such as a bank trust department, which usually bases its fees on the value of the account; still others might appoint their CPAs or an attorney who might charge their regular hourly rates.

Using an RLT to Plan for Possible Incapacity

Unlike a will, a revocable living trust can operate during your lifetime as well as after death. After a grantor's death, trustees act much like the executors of a will, but they don't have to go through the court probate process. They account to the remainder beneficiaries instead of to the court. "Remainder beneficiaries" are those who will receive the assets after the death of the grantor who established the trust – that is, they receive what remains in the trust estate upon the death of the grantor. In the case of a trust, the successor trustee is directed by instructions in the trust document as to what to do about the assets, such as distributing certain amounts to specified beneficiaries or providing for the trust to continue, or be subdivided into new trusts, for minor or disabled beneficiaries.

If the grantor/trustee of the trust is alive but incapacitated, the successor trustee might be specifically directed by the terms of the trust about how the grantor wishes his or her care to be managed. If you execute a trust with incapacity planning provisions, your instructions for care can be very detailed and contain specific wishes on exactly how, where and by whom you want to be cared for. For example, if you can afford care in your own home, then, subject to safety considerations, you can specify that you wish to be cared for at home and that you do not wish to be placed in a nursing home.

There is a discussion later about special needs trusts (SNTs) for disabled beneficiaries. SNT language is intended to assure that a disabled beneficiary is provided with goods and services that enhance the quality of his or her life. Revocable trusts that contain directions regarding the care of the grantor in the event of incapacity are analogous to SNTs. If the grantor no longer has the capacity to direct how he or she prefers to be cared for, the trust language can contain such provisions. An incapacitated grantor might be unable to manage his or her affairs, but might still enjoy restaurant outings and companions just as SNT beneficiaries do. These "incapacity planning" provisions can, for example, direct the trustee to hire an Aging Life geriatric care manager (GCM) who would develop a care plan for the grantor. The care plan might provide that home health aides be hired and that the grantor's care be actively monitored by the GCM – just as if the GCM were an adult daughter of the grantor.

Revocable living trusts can be amended or revoked by the grantor at any time as long as the grantor is mentally competent, just as others can execute new wills or codicils whenever they wish. Revocable Living Trusts are sometimes called simply "living" trusts because they become effective during the grantor's lifetime, unlike a trust established under the terms of a will after death (testamentary trusts as mentioned earlier).

If the grantor has included such specific instructions for care in the event of incapacity, those instructions are binding on the trustee. If the grantor for reasons of safety or affordability must be placed in a nursing home or other facility, he or she can specify which facility is preferred; the trust document can further specify that a geriatric care manager shall provide for frequent, even daily, care monitoring to prevent abuse or neglect (see later discussion in Elder Abuse and Neglect section.)

Example: Directing Your Own Care in Event of Incapacity

Example: An elderly woman with substantial assets has two children who live out of state. She emphatically wants to be able to live in her own home until her death; she does not want to go to a nursing home if she develops something like Alzheimer's Disease. She also wants to leave an inheritance to her family, but her priority is for her own assets to be spent on her own quality of life before that of the next generation. It's her money. Her trustee is also instructed to make annual (tax) exclusion gifts to her children as long as doing so does not jeopardize her own care.

Eventually she develops dementia. Her named successor trustee takes over the management of the trust "box" and follows the directions set forth in her trust document. The trustee's first task is to hire a geriatric care manager to develop and implement a care plan for the grantor. The geriatric care manager hired by the trustee places and supervises home health aides who care for the grantor 24/7. The trustee arranges for any needed help from accountants to landscapers to furnace repair people.

Companions are hired who take the grantor and her home health aide to the supermarket, out to favorite restaurants and to visit the mall to see the holiday lights. They listen patiently and respond appropriately to the grantor's stories, no matter how often she has told them. Sleeping and eating schedules are set according to the grantor's preferences. She does not have to adhere to an institutional schedule. Every afternoon she is served her favorite snack – what she calls ice cream but which is actually frozen yogurt. She is safe and content. Just because she suffers from dementia does not mean she's oblivious to her surroundings, her care or what she eats. Without such a trust, and with no geographically available family members, that woman would have had no alternative but to go to a nursing home. After her death, the successor trustee would distribute her estate as provided in the trust just as would an executor under a will.

Although RLTs are widely used, in some states, such as New York and New Jersey, they are not used as often. Check with your estate planning or elder law attorney if you think you might benefit from an RLT.

Disadvantages of a Revocable Living Trust

An estate plan based on a revocable living trust will likely be more costly than a plan based on a will. Retitling your assets can also be cumbersome, although your attorney should be able to do most of that work. In most but not all states, probate can be fairly simple and inexpensive. If probate avoidance is your only reason for considering an RLT then an RLT-based plan is probably not worth the money and effort.

Irrevocable Trusts

Irrevocable trusts cannot be changed or revoked. An irrevocable trust can be created during the grantor's lifetime or it can be created as a testamentary trust within the language of a regular will. If it is incorporated into the language of a will, it is irrevocable because by the time it is comes into effect, the testator is deceased and can't revoke it. An irrevocable trust is created in order to effectively cause the assets in the trust to be unreachable by anyone except those explicitly identified in the trust.

Irrevocable trusts are often used by the wealthy to reduce estate taxes and to transfer wealth to the next generation while minimizing such taxes. They are also used by people at the other end of the economic spectrum to protect assets in the event that Medicaid might ever be needed.

If you think you might be a candidate for an irrevocable trust, consult with your tax or elder law attorney. www.naela.org

Irrevocable Life Insurance Trusts (ILIT)

Life Insurance Trusts are commonly used to shelter assets from estate taxes if it is set up at least three years prior to the grantor's death. An example of a life insurance trust would be a trust created by a grantor with instructions to an independent trustee to purchase life insurance on the life of the grantor naming the trust as beneficiary of the life insurance proceeds. The trust document itself then provides what will actually be done with those proceeds when the insured grantor dies. Beneficiaries of such trusts are usually spouses and children, but they are also very useful in providing for the special needs of a disabled beneficiary. Whereas the grantor might "give away" a large sum of money for premiums, the life insurance proceeds could amount to millions of dollars which are NOT considered part of the grantor's taxable estate. The proceeds are in fact actually owned by the trust without any estate or significant income tax implications. Example: Your trustee pays $100,000 to purchase a $1,000,000 policy on your life and then you die. The $1 million death benefit is paid to the Trustee of the irrevocable trust for the benefit of those you have designated and therefore is not counted as an asset included in your estate for the purpose of calculating estate taxes. There are sophisticated methods of providing for premium payments without incurring estate or gift tax liability. Discuss with your estate planning or elder law attorney.

Asset Protection Trusts for Long-Term Care Medicaid Planning

Irrevocable trusts for Medicaid planning are used to "start the clock ticking" on the five-year look-back period for transfers of assets for less than fair market value (see later Medicaid discussion). The Medicaid applicant can be penalized for such transfers, or gifts, by a delay in receipt of Medicaid benefits even if the applicant is otherwise eligible for Medicaid. The beneficiary of a typical asset protection trust may not receive distributions of principal from the trust, but is usually permitted to receive income earned on the trust's assets.

When assets are transferred into an "asset protection" irrevocable trust, they are "given away" under the rules of Medicaid. Example: A widow transfers money into an irrevocable trust for the benefit of her children but she retains the right to receive income earned on the assets. The assets in the irrevocable trust will in most jurisdictions not count as a current asset of the widow. However, even if she is otherwise eligible for LTC Medicaid, she will be penalized if she funded the asset protection trust within five years of her application. If after the five-year period she does qualify for Medicaid, he income she receives from the trust will count as income that must be paid to the nursing home.

These trusts are designed to prevent assets from being considered as owned by or available to a Medicaid applicant. Trust assets can ultimately be left to others in accordance with the provisions of the trust. Irrevocable asset protection trusts are subject to myriad legal subtleties and, depending on the circumstances, can be ineffective in some jurisdictions.

SPECIAL NEEDS TRUST (SNT)

Special Needs Trust Overview

A Special Needs trust (SNT) is a trust established for the benefit of a disabled individual for the purpose of providing goods and services **other than** basic health, maintenance and support. An underlying principle guiding the drafting of SNTs is that the beneficiary's basic support needs will be met by public benefits programs such as SSI, SSDI, Medicaid, (discussed later) and Medicare (discussed earlier). Many beneficiaries qualify for all four of these programs. SSI and Medicaid, however, are "means-tested." Beneficiaries under such programs must have almost no income or assets. Rather than providing for basic health and support, a SNT provides for everything else. It provides life-enhancing goods and services that would otherwise be provided by the beneficiary's family members or by charitable entities. If no family members or charities are available, the beneficiary will survive, but will not have the extras and luxuries that make life much more pleasant.

Because the assets used by the trustee of the SNT to provide benefits do not belong to the beneficiary personally - they belong to the trust - the beneficiary is not considered "over asset" for eligibility purposes. The trust may contain provisions severely limiting or even prohibiting expenditures of trust assets for the beneficiary's basic health and support needs. SNTs typically give the trustee absolute discretion with respect to making, or not making, distributions for the benefit of the disabled beneficiary. The trust language should make clear that the purpose of the trust is to supplement, not supplant, the public benefits.

Family members regularly visit their disabled loved ones, rent wheelchair vans to take them on outings, provide for regular dental and vision care, and generally do whatever they can to enhance their loved ones' quality of life. But what happens to a beneficiary when mom and dad die, when siblings move away or become just too busy to make daily visits? What the beneficiary needs is a "stand-in" for mom or dad when they are no longer able to provide such services.

That stand-in can be an SNT. The trustee of the SNT manages money given to the SNT by lifetime gifts or upon the death of someone who wishes to provide for the special needs of the beneficiary. An SNT document should be prepared with the specific needs of the particular beneficiary in mind. A beneficiary crippled by cerebral palsy could benefit from a wheelchair van, or encouragement to the trustee to rent one using assets of the SNT. That same beneficiary might enjoy electronic or digital equipment. Some developmentally disabled beneficiaries especially enjoy such things as outings to favorite restaurants and even trips to Disney World with paid companions.

Family members and well-intentioned others should ***never*** give or leave money directly to a disabled individual who receives, or who might in the future receive, means-tested public benefits. Funds should always be given or left to an SNT for the benefit of such beneficiary.

SNTs are often established and funded by parents or other relatives during their own lifetimes. They are also often established under the Last Will and Testament (or the after-death portion of an RLT) of a parent, grandparent or other person who cares about the well-being of the beneficiary.

Special Needs Trusts are not, however, solely for the benefit of younger beneficiaries or the adult child beneficiaries of older parents. Many adult caregivers of beloved relatives, such as a daughter who has been caring for her elderly, frail mother, provide in their own wills or RLTs for SNTs to be established for the benefit of that frail elderly loved one. After daughter's death, her mother may well find herself in a nursing home. Daughter's SNT for mom can assure that mom receives frequent visitors and care-monitors and is treated to her favorite foods and whatever other life enhancing goods and services she might enjoy.

Third Party SNTs

Any Special Needs Trust (SNT) established during the lifetime of a grantor who is not the disabled beneficiary, and which is funded with that person's assets, is known as a "third party" SNT. SNTs established under a will or RLT and funded after the death of the individual whose money is used to fund the SNT are also third party trusts. A third party is anyone other than the beneficiary. In this context, the beneficiary is known as the "first party."

Third party SNTs can be completely exempt from being counted as assets available to the disabled beneficiary. The trustee must be careful not to make distributions directly to the beneficiary or other distributions that might disqualify the beneficiary from receiving certain benefits. With respect to both SSI and Medicaid, there can be some variation among different jurisdictions as to how some distributions will be viewed. SNTs are usually drafted by elder law attorneys who are familiar with how the trustee should handle distributions. Third party trusts can provide that any assets remaining in the SNT upon the death of the beneficiary can be distributed to other persons named by the grantor/testator, such as siblings of the beneficiary. To locate an elder law attorney in your jurisdiction, go to www.naela.org.

First Party or Self-Settled SNTs

What if Uncle Harry didn't get the message and left the disabled beneficiary $100,000 in his will? Or what if the beneficiary was injured in an accident and stands to receive a cash settlement? In these situations, an elder law attorney should be contacted immediately to prepare a special type of SNT that will allow such lump sum payments to benefit the disabled individual without public benefits disqualification.

In cases such as these, the cash in question is owned by the disabled beneficiary, i.e., the "first party." Under the regular rules, that cash would disqualify him or her from continued receipt of public benefits because he or she would be "over assets" - meaning that he or she owned too much money. Absent intervention by the Congress, the beneficiary would just have to spend down the money until it was gone and then go back on public benefits. However, the Congress enacted special exceptions for these situations.

Under 42 U.S.C. Section 1396p(d)(4)(A), a parent, grandparent, guardian or a court can create a SNT for the beneficiary and use that beneficiary's own money (the inheritance, the settlement, etc.) to fund it without the transfer being considered a disqualifying gift and without the assets held in the new SNT being considered "available" to the beneficiary. This type of SNT must include a provision that upon the death of the beneficiary, assets remaining in the SNT must be repaid to Medicaid up to the value of the benefits Medicaid provided. These trusts are referred to as "Medicaid Payback Trusts" or as "(d)(4)(A) trusts" - interchangeable terms. Medicaid Payback trusts can only be established for disabled persons under age 65.

For older beneficiaries, and for beneficiaries whose lump sum is so small that it doesn't warrant the establishment of a separate trust, there is another exception to the general rule that any assets of the beneficiary are disqualifying for public benefits. These are known as (d)(4)(C) or "pooled" trusts. A pooled trust is one established by a non-profit community group for the benefit of disabled individuals. Money contributed to a pooled trust can be held in a special subaccount for the benefit of the person whose money funded the subaccount. In some jurisdictions, (d)(4)(c) trusts must be funded before the beneficiary turns 65. Such subaccounts can be created by a parent, grandparent, guardian, court or by the beneficiary himself. The trustees of the pooled trust will manage and make distributions from the subaccount for the benefit of the disabled person during his or her lifetime. Funds remaining in a deceased beneficiary's subaccount must either be paid over to Medicaid or transferred into a general account of the pooled trust to be available to benefit any beneficiary of the pooled trust.

MEDICAID FOR LONG-TERM CARE (LTC)

Long-Term Care Medicaid Overview

It still surprises many people that neither Medicare nor Medigap policies cover most care in a long-term care facility or nursing home. Private pay long-term care nursing home costs can very quickly use up one's life savings. If you cannot afford the fees as a private pay patient, you may need Medicaid. The average annual cost of private pay long-term care in a nursing home is $87,000.

Individuals who require long-term care are those who need help with performing basic Activities of Daily Living (ADLs) such as bathing, dressing, eating, toileting/continence issues, and transferring (getting in and out of bed or chair). Help with these ADLs is called "custodial care."

Many people are especially shocked to learn that care in a nursing home for an illness such as Alzheimer's Disease is not covered by Medicare. As noted earlier, Medicare pays only for limited skilled nursing home care, such as physical therapy. Long-term care is not skilled care. The costs of long-term care can bankrupt families.

Medicaid LTC Basic Rules

Medicaid is a joint federal and state funded program enacted in 1965. Although the programs are run by individual states, they must all conform to basic standards established by the Centers for Medicare and Medicaid (CMS) under federal statutes enacted by the Congress. This discussion is based on federal law and uses Virginia (home of the author) as its example state. This discussion also relates only to the special Medicaid rules governing long-term care. Regular Medicaid (as distinct from long-term care Medicaid) for individuals living in the community has some different provisions.

You can qualify for long-term care Medicaid when your income is below a specified level and you have minimal assets, usually $2000 or less, as well as not being able to perform at least two activities of daily living (ADLs). However, states have broad leeway as to how they implement their long-term care Medicaid programs. Court decisions in cases challenging various state procedures have produced contradictory results as to how certain rules will apply in different states.

Therefore, if you or any loved one might ever require Long-Term Care (LTC) Medicaid, consultation with an experienced elder law attorney is absolutely essential. As noted, you can locate an elder law attorney in your jurisdiction at the website of the National Academy of Elder Law Attorneys (NAELA) www.naela.org. To find individual attorneys in your local jurisdiction on this website, click on the red "Find an Attorney" button in the upper right hand corner of your screen. Then, on the page that comes up on your screen, scroll down to "Find an Attorney." (And, p.s., I have not actively been associated with an elder law firm since 2005 and am not, as noted previously, intending to give legal advice).

Medicaid LTC Eligibility - Income and Assets

Many seniors who do not ordinarily live near the poverty line can quickly become financially devastated by an injury or illness requiring long-term care. As mentioned, to qualify for Medicaid for long-term care, individuals must have as little as $2000 or less in countable assets, and receive income which is insufficient to cover the costs of their care.

Some states have income caps for eligibility whereas others allow you to "spend down," meaning, as a practical matter, that as long as your cost of care exceeds your income you can become Medicaid eligible.

Generally, all income received by a spouse who is institutionalized must be paid to the nursing home except for a small allowance which varies by state law. For instance, in the state of Virginia, an institutionalized spouse (IS) may keep a personal needs allowance of $40 a month. The spouse who continues to reside in the community, called the community spouse (CS), however, may keep all income he or she receives in his or her own name with no upper limit, as discussed below in the Medicaid for married couples section.

Some states, known as "income cap" states, provide that individuals whose income exceeds a certain level cannot qualify for LTC Medicaid. In states with such "income caps," Medicaid qualification can be obtained by using what are known as "Miller trusts," a name derived from a court case in which it was shown that individuals subject to an income cap could find themselves in an impossible position. Creative attorneys proposed, and the court agreed, that an individual's "excess" income could be put into a special trust so that the income they actually receive, and thus pay to the nursing home, is lower than the cap. Medicaid ultimately recovers Miller trust funds. For example, prior to Miller trusts, an individual with $5000 per month income - high by most standards - could be above the income cap but still not have enough income to pay for a $7000 per month nursing home.

Long-term care Medicaid laws and rules can be as complex as the Internal Revenue Code. If you actually think you or a family member is going to need long-term care, you should contact an elder law attorney in your jurisdiction as soon as possible. Elder law attorneys can help navigate the murky Medicaid rules and assist families to protect assets which, in turn, can be used for the needs of the patients or other family members.

Gift-Giving to Reduce Assets - The "Five-Year Look Back"

Although the details of Medicaid rules vary from state to state, they are all governed by the federal framework embodied in statute and implemented by CMS. One rule that is common to virtually all states involves what is known as the "five-year look back" for asset transfers for less than fair market value made by an individual or his/her spouse. This rule applies to all LTC Medicaid applicants, both married and unmarried. If an individual or his or her spouse gave away any assets within five years of an application for long-term care Medicaid, a severe penalty period, i.e., a waiting period for Medicaid coverage, will be imposed. There are some exceptions to the rule that transferring money or a house will trigger a penalty, such as to a spouse or disabled child. Check with an elder law attorney to find out more about what current allowable exceptions are.

Medicaid in each state will compute a dollar amount, which is supposed to be the average monthly cost of a nursing home in that area. They will use that amount to compute the penalty period resulting from a transfer of assets for less than fair market value. For example, in Virginia the average amount for a private pay nursing home is about $6,500 per month. If you or your spouse gave any assets away in the five years prior to a Virginia application date, Medicaid divides the dollar amount you gave away by the $6,500 "average cost of private pay." The resulting number is the "penalty period," i.e., the number of months you will have to wait for Medicaid coverage. If multiple transfers are made during the five-year look back period, they are added together to form one grand total into which the average cost of private pay is divided. The penalty period *begins with the month you would otherwise have been eligible for Medicaid based on your income (insufficient to pay for nursing home care), assets (as low as $2000) and inability to perform a minimum number of activities of daily living (ADLs).*

This means that the penalty period begins to run when you are already indigent and in the nursing home. The rule is designed to be so draconian that individuals often must have family members return gifts prior to the Medicaid application process. This is known as "curing" the transfer; procedures vary from state to state. These rules exist so that people will be discouraged from giving away assets to relatives and then asking Medicaid to pay for their long-term care costs.

It is also true in a (hopefully) small number of places that Medicaid-funded care is inferior to the care provided to private-pay patients. Many private-pay patients or their families choose care in nursing homes that are completely private pay and thus accept no Medicaid patients at all.

Verification

Some jurisdictions are requiring Medicaid applicants to produce five years' worth of financial records. Then they question the applicant about withdrawals as small as $300. Did you give this away? If not, what did you spend it on? If the records show a deposit whose source is not obvious, Medicaid will ask for details to determine whether the money came from a sale or other transfer "for less than fair market value." Answering such questions can be impossible for most people. This type of detailed "verification" process is a relatively new phenomenon which has drawn the attention of elder law attorneys who might challenge it in those jurisdictions that are applying it.

Many families share household costs. Ex: Mom and daughter have a joint account and over the years daughter has written a few checks to pay bills that are her own, and she has used some of her own cash from her sole account for things for her mom etc. Even these small things that don't seem like a big deal can cause mayhem when applying for Medicaid. Expenses for the Medicaid applicant must be kept separate, at least for 5 years prior to applying for Medicaid. Try if at all possible never to use cash from a future applicant's bank account. Every penny in theory has to be accounted for as being for the primary benefit of the applicant. Cash is very hard to track unless you are 100% solid about keeping every receipt you have ever gotten. Even in that case, the amount of photo-copying you may have to do to submit all the "evidence" could overwhelm you *and* the Medicaid worker who has to sort through it!

Life Estate: A Short Cut Through The 5 Year Lookback?

As stated above, you can't just give your adult child your home for $1 in order to save it from being counted as your asset for Medicaid purposes. However, with the help of an elder law attorney, some people are transferring their house deed to their adult children (or other family member) while maintaining a "life estate". A life estate is where you sell, or give someone your house, except that you have the right to remain there until you die or move. It is a way to keep the family homestead in the family so to speak for those who feel that is important in case they ever need Medicaid. If you don't need Medicaid for 5 years after the deed transfer, then the home belongs to your relative and you get to own the right to live there until you die or move. If you need Medicaid within 5 years of the transfer, Medicaid calculates the age of the tenant and the value of the house and assigns a value, (like an actuary table of sorts) --such as- wife is 80, how long is she expected to live, and then decides- well she "gave away" ___% which equals $___ triggering a look back penalty for the amount they apportioned as being given away or gifted.

If you fully transfer the deed without keeping a life estate interest, the house can't be used for Medicaid repayment, just like giving your kid $100,000- it's gone. Medicaid gets to count the whole amount as a gift, use it for penalty now but can't recoup later from a sale of the property because it isn't owned by the Medicaid beneficiary. When people started doing this to "save the family homestead", through a Life Estate, Medicaid had to come up with a way try to mitigate that they can't get paid back as much because the house goes to the kids upon death of the parent, so they use a certain % to count for penalty.

Adult Child Caregiver Exception

One express exception to the rule that a Medicaid applicant will be penalized for making gifts within five years of the Medicaid application date is known as the "caregiver child" exception. This exception provides that an applicant can transfer his home to an adult child who lived with him in that home and provided care that kept him out of a nursing home for at least two years. Therefore, Dad's gift of his home to his daughter who lived with him and took care of him for several years, at least two of which were years when Dad could not bathe or dress himself, is an exempt transfer.

Elements of the caregiver child exception must be verified. When the caregiver child first moves into Dad's house, his doctor should write a letter confirming that Dad cannot live alone safely. As Dad's condition declines to the point where he can no longer perform at least two activities of daily living (ADLs), daughter should obtain another letter from Dad's doctor confirming this. Daughter must also be able to demonstrate that she was Dad's primary caregiver for at least two years in which he couldn't perform at least two ADLs, and that without her care, he would have had to go into a nursing home. Different jurisdictions will require different levels of verification. Proof that daughter had to cut back or even quit her employment in order to care for Dad is very persuasive. Medicaid will look to see if daughter hired 24/7 caregivers for Dad in which case, her claim to being his primary caregiver would require other types of proof.

Note that the caregiver child exception applies only to situations in which the adult child moves into the *parent's* home to provide care. More often it is the parent who moves into the adult child's home. However, depending on jurisdiction, an adult child caregiver who is providing care in his/her own home can offset some of what would otherwise be a substantial disincentive to providing such care. It is in everyone's interest that Dad be kept out of a nursing home for as long as possible.

The question arises: What financial incentive, equivalent to the express caregiver child exception described above, is available to Dad and you, his daughter, when Dad is being cared for in your home? You are aware that the time will come when you may be foregoing employment income and will be "on call" 24 hours a day. Dad knows this and wants to compensate you in some way. Since you are not providing care in a home owned by Dad, he has no home to give you. But there are steps that can be taken, in most jurisdictions that will allow Dad to compensate you for your care. Both you and Dad recognize that he will probably have to go to a nursing home one day, but he'd like to forestall that day as long as possible. What might you and Dad do?

First, when Dad moves in, he becomes the equivalent of a roommate. Let's say he has suffered a stroke which has resulted in some permanent, though not extensive, paralysis. You agree that he can live with you and your husband. He sells his house and moves in with you. He can still manage pretty well on his own so far. Dad insists on "paying his own way." You add up the monthly household expenses, including mortgage, taxes, utilities, maintenance, food and household supplies and Dad chips in his one third. You keep *all* records of such expenses because if Dad has to apply for Medicaid anytime in the next five years he/you will have to prove that his checks to you were not gifts but simply his share of the household expenses "hotchpot." Verify with your tax advisor that Dad's contributions to the hotchpot are not taxable income to you any more than college roommates' sharing of living expenses would be.

Then Dad declines further. He has money from the sale of his house. You arrange for a home health aide to come in every morning to help Dad with bathing, toileting and dressing. The home health aide gives Dad his breakfast, cleans up and leaves lunch for him in the refrigerator. The fees for the aide are paid by Dad.

Dad begins to exhibit early signs of Alzheimer's Disease. He calls you at your office practically every hour. The home health aide says he has become very difficult to deal with. You seem to be the only person he will cooperate with in bathing, toileting and dressing. You decide you have no choice but to quit your job to take care of Dad.

Meanwhile, Dad still has more than $100,000 left from the sale of his house. He says he wants you to have it because you are taking care of him. If he gives you all or part of that money, will it be considered a gift? Will the transfer be considered disqualifying for Medicaid purposes and thus subject Dad to a significant financial penalty? Of course, jurisdiction will again be relevant. In many cases, however, a transfer of a lump sum to an adult child caregiver will be considered a gift. Courts have reasoned that services performed by family members are presumed to be gifts. But presumptions can be rebutted. It is frequently acceptable that Dad and daughter can enter into a binding contract (which MUST be drafted with the help of an elder law attorney) whereby Dad agrees to compensate you for your services.

What should be in the contract? First of all, it probably should not involve a lump sum. Ordinarily, payment for services is made when the services are rendered. Thus, an agreement whereby Dad promises to pay a certain amount per week or per month for your caregiving services, and then actually makes those periodic payments on schedule – with no lump sum involved – will be good evidence that his payments to you were not gift-giving transfers. Dad's payments must be based on the fair market value of your services. How do you know what amount Medicaid will consider fair value for your services? You will probably have to collect a variety of fee schedules from care providers in your area such as Aging Life Care managers, home health aides, assisted living facilities and so forth. Then, with the help of the attorney who is assisting you and Dad, you stir all those numbers around to come up with a reasonable dollar amount to put in the caregiving agreement. The agreement will specify the types of services you will provide and how much and how often you will be paid. Medicaid might inquire whether you have paid income tax on the funds received. Medicaid has been known to argue that such payments were gifts solely because the adult child could not show that she had paid income and payroll taxes on them. Check with your tax advisor to determine if tax is actually due; exceptions might apply.

Again, when these techniques are appropriate, you must document, document and document some more. Keep household receipts. Keep copies of all checks. Keep records of when respite aides were hired and how much they were paid. Keep records of all of Dad's other expenses such as medical co-pays, Medigap premiums, prescriptions, items of clothing and so forth. Keep track of Dad's payments for home safety items such as grab bars and "baby" monitors. Keep track of both Dad's and your bank records and tax returns. Requests for documentation by Medicaid can be very onerous. Collecting and organizing documentation along the way can vastly simplify your life if and when the time comes that you need to help Dad to qualify for nursing home Medicaid.

When the time comes that Dad can no longer remain safely in your home, he will enter a nursing home. If his countable resources (cash) equal $2000 or less, he will be immediately eligible for Medicaid. If he has more than that amount, consider prepaying a burial plan for him and buying items such as clothing he will likely need in the future. Anything left will be used to pay the nursing home. Being able to pay a nursing home for several months of private pay can also result in your having a better selection of nursing homes.

Disabled Child Exception

Mrs. Ayres and her son, Charlie, reside in a small condo that is within walking distance of their neighborhood shopping area. Charlie, 45, is developmentally disabled. He receives SSDI and Medicare based on his late father's work record. Mrs. Ayres has been a stay-at-home mom, taking care of Charlie. Charlie has benefited from local programs for the disabled. He can walk by himself to the community center where his group meets and to neighborhood restaurants and shops. He can manage small amounts of cash to buy food; he can operate a microwave. He would not be able to manage a bank account or buy a new TV. He is not neat, although he is not a hoarder.

When Mrs. Ayres becomes ill, she realizes that there is no one available who could provide Charlie with the care and assistance that she provides him. She also knows, as her health declines, that he can't take care of her. She can see the day coming when she will have to enter a nursing home.

But what of Charlie? Mrs. Ayres owns the condo free and clear and has several hundred thousand dollars from her late husband's life insurance. She wants Charlie to be able to continue living in the condo but he will need help with basic finances, not to mention housekeeping matters. As we have seen, gift-giving by a Medicaid applicant can be disastrous. However, when enacting the Medicaid gift-penalty language of the Medicaid statute, the Congress expressly provided an exception to the general rule in the case of transfers to or for the benefit of a disabled child. Mrs. Ayres can transfer ownership of her condo together with available liquid assets directly to Charlie without worrying about a Medicaid penalty. In this case, however, rather than transferring the assets directly to Charlie, she can establish a "third-party SNT" (see discussion above) for Charlie. The trust can include provisions to assist Charlie, such as hiring a case manager to keep an eye on how he's doing, a housekeeper to come in on a regular basis, and any extra one-time expenses he cannot cover with his SSDI payment. The trust can provide that any assets remaining upon Charlie's death should be distributed to whatever support group is assisting him at the time of his death. The community group has assured Mrs. Ayres that it will continue to provide social support to Charlie and be alert to any needs that might arise. After Mrs. Ayres enters the nursing home on Medicaid, Charlie's community support group arranges for him to visit her at least once a week.

Community LTC Medicaid Waivers

Traditionally, Medicaid paid for long-term care costs ONLY in nursing homes. Today, Medicaid allows more diverse services and support for individuals living at home by "waiving" the need to get those services in a nursing home. This is what is meant by the term "Medicaid Waivers." In some jurisdictions, Medicaid waivers allow Medicaid coverage for patients in assisted living facilities, and not just skilled nursing homes. Each state has different income requirements. Individuals still need to meet certain level-of-care requirements to receive the Medicaid Waivers, but the program allows them to remain living in the community. **Depending on your state**, Medicaid Waivers may even pay for service providers in your home who are unlicensed or are family members.

Some of the services Medicaid Waivers will pay for, depending on the state, are: case management (i.e. supports and service coordination), homemaker, home health aide, personal care, adult day health care, and respite care, a personal emergency response system, medication monitoring, transition services and coordination, environmental modifications and assistive technology.

LTC MEDICAID RULES FOR MARRIED COUPLES

There are special Medicaid rules for married couples which differ from those for individuals. Congress created a set of rules which are designed to enable spouses who will still be living at home to remain there and support themselves while their spouses are in a Medicaid-paid nursing home. Courts recognize that Medicaid planning, can be accomplished by those who are knowledgeable enough to seek legal counsel before either spouse becomes ill. They reason that equal protection principles should allow those less knowledgeable to benefit from Congress' intent that nursing home costs should not land a community spouse on the street.

The at-home spouse is called the **"community spouse" (CS)** because he or she is still living in the community. The spouse in the nursing home is known as the **"institutionalized spouse" (IS).**

These special Medicaid rules are designed to prevent the impoverishment of the community spouse. The community spouse may keep up to a specified maximum of "countable" assets. The maximum amount which can be kept is currently $119,220. That amount changes each year. Some states allow the CS to keep only the lesser of one-half of all of his/her/their countable assets, up to the specified maximum. The CS can also keep assets designated as exempt, as discussed below.

The Protected Resource Amount (PRA) refers to what dollar amount can be retained by the spouse who is not going into a nursing home under Medicaid. If one spouse is applying for Medicaid to cover nursing home fees, and the couple's countable assets are between the minimum and maximum amount, the spouse staying at home will be able to keep half. The current minimum that can be retained by the community spouse is $23,844. In Virginia, the maximum is one-half of all of the countable assets or $119,220, whichever is lower. Some states automatically allow the community spouse to retain all countable assets up to the maximum $119,220. The maximum amount of countable assets that can be retained by the CS must be computed in accordance with detailed rules. If the community spouse does not have even as much as the minimum amount, he or she will be able to keep what is available, but no additional funds will be provided by the government.

Assets/Resources: Snapshot Date

In addition to the dollar value assets, the community spouse may also keep one car, a primary residence, and some other assets which are exempt. These spousal rules are quite different from the rules applied to a single person for whom almost nothing is exempt.

When knowledgeably applied, these rules can permit an institutionalized spouse to qualify for Medicaid while often preserving for the CS, in one form or another, the entire net worth of the spouses. Again, to navigate the complex rules, contact a member of the National Academy of Elder Law Attorneys. www.naela.org.

Medicaid determines the amount of a married couple's "countable assets" by using a dollar amount to represent the total assets, both countable and exempt, belonging to the couple as of a "snapshot date." This snapshot date is the first day of the first month in which a person was in a facility for at least 30 days and/or is expected to remain institutionalized indefinitely. For example, a husband enters a nursing home on October 9th and expects to remain there indefinitely. The snapshot date will be October 1st. If he had gone into the hospital in September and was then transferred to the nursing home in October, the snapshot date would be September 1st.

Community spouses in several jurisdictions are allowed to "just say no" to making his or her assets available for the support of the IS. This procedure is known as "spousal refusal." Community spouses (who say no), or their estates, might later be sued by Medicaid for the amount of benefits provided to the IS. These "spousal refusals" and subsequent lawsuits are grounded in laws requiring spouses to support each other. Check with your elder law attorney to determine whether spousal refusal is allowed in your state and, if so, how it works as a practical matter.

Assets: Countable or Exempt

Medicaid counts every asset possessed by either or both of the spouses as of the snapshot date. It then disregards "exempt" assets such as the home occupied by the community spouse. In 2017 the community spouse will then be allowed to keep at least one-half of all countable assets up to the maximum allowance of $120,900. There is also a Minimum resource allowance of $24,180, whereby if the lesser of one half of the assets falls below, the community spouse can retain the minimum amount. These amounts can change annually.

Consider a Northern Virginia married couple with $400,000 in countable assets all jointly titled. The husband's health is declining and he needs nursing home care. He will need to apply for Medicaid long-term care benefits. For 2017, his wife can keep $120,900 of that $400,000, which is the lesser of one-half of the countable assets as of the snapshot date, ($200,000). In planning ahead, they know the remaining $279,100 of *countable* assets must be spent on something without being given away. Their goal is to spend that amount in a way that will enhance the financial security of the CS.

Assets which are exempt are the home occupied by the community spouse, one car of any value, furniture, furnishings and personal effects that are not extremely valuable, and prepaid burial plans.

Common planning techniques include using excess countable assets to pay off a mortgage, repair the house, buy a new car, pre-pay funeral plans and take other actions to protect the community spouse. By installing a new furnace and replacing the windows of the old house, for example, countable assets such as cash are converted to an exempt asset, i.e., the house. Utility expenses will be reduced, and the house will be more valuable if the CS later sells it.

Depending on jurisdiction, some more sophisticated planning tools can include very carefully structured annuities and irrevocable trusts. Do not attempt these techniques without the help of an elder law attorney. Remember that each state has varying Medicaid rules.

The Community Spouse Protected Resource Amount (CSPRA) is the amount of countable resources the community spouse is allowed to possess, up to the maximum of $120,900, as of the institutionalized spouse's eligibility date. These assets are also known as the Community Spouse Resource Allowance (CSRA).

Minimum Monthly Maintenance Needs Allowance: The MMMNA

Some community spouses do not have enough assets to worry about spending down, but they are concerned about having enough income to live on. As mentioned above, any income the nursing home spouse receives, such as from Social Security, must go to the nursing home to help offset what Medicaid is paying from tax dollars. However, there is an exception to this rule. It is called the "Minimum (or "Maximum") Monthly Maintenance Needs Allowance" (MMMNA) for the community spouse.

If the community spouse does not have enough monthly income of his or her own, he or she may get some of the income the nursing home spouse receives before it goes to help pay for the nursing home care. The *minimum* MMMNA for all states except Alaska and Hawaii (which are usually a few hundred dollars higher) will be $3,022.50

The *minimum* MMMNA in 2017 is $2,002.50. If income in the name of a community spouse, such as her social security benefit, is below the minimum level, she is entitled to an allowance from her institutionalized spouse's income to bring her up to that level. By showing need, the Community Spouse (CS) might be entitled to an allowance from her Institutionalized Spouse (IS) in an amount that can bring her income up to the maximum. A CS can retain all income received in his or her own name with no maximum. A CS who already receives income in excess of $3,022.50 will not be entitled to any income allowance from the IS. The law also provides that a community spouse might qualify to keep extra countable assets which, when invested, would bring his or her income up to the allowed MMMNA level. This last rule is increasingly rare in practice.

The community spouse rules result in the use of tax dollars to pay for long-term care in order to prevent the impoverishment of community spouses. The wealthy in the United States can typically afford their long-term care costs. The already-poor can easily qualify for Medicaid. Without the protective Medicaid rules for spouses, it would be only the middle class that would have to give up all their savings and the family home to pay for long-term care.

Example: A Married Couple Achieves Medicaid Eligibility

For illustration purposes the following example is extremely simplified and numbers are rounded. Each individual situation must be analyzed to determine how to maximize the financial security of a spouse who remains at home when her spouse becomes institutionalized in a long-term care facility:

Helen and Joe Miller have lived in their comfortable home for 50 years. The home is worth about $180,000. Helen receives $1400 per month in Social Security. Joe has both Social Security and a pension totaling $2600 per month. They also have savings of about $175,000, and a 10-year old car. They have a line of credit with an outstanding balance of $7,000 from a loan they took out six years ago, to help their grandson with his student loan repayment. With no mortgage, other than the small line of credit, Helen and Joe have lived comfortably on their combined income of $4000 per month.

After a year or so of increasing memory and confusion issues, Joe was diagnosed with Alzheimer's Disease. His decline has been rapid. Helen cares for him at home with no help. She is 5'3" and weighs 135 pounds; Joe is 6'2" and weighs more than 190 pounds. In the middle of a recent freezing winter night, Joe left the house in his pajamas and walked for 10 blocks in his bare feet before he was spotted by a police officer. He was taken to the emergency room with frostbite. Helen awakened a few hours later, found him gone and called the police. Helen and Joe were soon reunited at the emergency room, but Helen knew she was not going to be able to restrain Joe in the future. Changing his diapers and trying to clean him was also becoming virtually impossible. It was time for Joe to go to a nursing home.

Nursing homes in Joe's and Helen's area cost, on average, about $6500 per month, $2500 per month more than their combined monthly income. Even if they spent all of their $175,000 nest egg on Joe's care, the money would last just over two years, and Helen would have nothing left for emergencies such as car repairs and home maintenance.

Helen and Joe had done everything right. They had worked hard, paid off their house, and set aside a comfortable nest egg. They kept their expenses low. Now Helen was looking at nursing home costs of $78,000 per year. Impossible. Helen was distraught. It was just such situations, however, that had prompted the Congress to enact the nursing home

Medicaid provisions designed to prevent the impoverishment of spouses like Helen when their ill spouses required nursing home care.

Applying the Medicaid asset and income rules discussed above, Joe will be able to qualify for Medicaid without impoverishing Helen. First, Helen can keep her own $1400 per month income. Ordinarily, all of Joe's $2600 per month income would go to the nursing home. However, the minimum monthly maintenance needs allowance (MMMNA) is **$2,002.50**. Helen receives only $1400 in her own name. Thus, Helen will be entitled to receive a $602.50 allowance from her husband's income to bring her total monthly income up to $2,002.50.

As to assets, assume that Helen and Joe reside in a jurisdiction that permits them to retain up to the maximum amount of countable assets – that is, a "resource allowance" of $120,900.00.

That means that Joe cannot qualify for Medicaid until the "extra" $54,100, ($175,000 nest egg less $120,900 resource allowance) is gone. Helen could simply pay the private pay rate for Joe until that money is gone. Or she could develop a plan to use that extra $54,100 to improve her financial security in light of the fact that she will be living on half of the household income she and Joe had received as a couple. She can make expenditures that will have the effect of reducing her monthly bills and increasing the value of the exempt assets she's allowed to keep. First, she should pay off the $7000 line of credit, thereby eliminating the monthly mortgage payment. The car is exempt. Her furniture and furnishings are exempt. The prepaid funeral plans and home improvements are exempt. She can install a new heating and air conditioning system and replace the windows to reduce her utility costs. She can buy a fuel-efficient "new" used car to replace the 10-year-old car that constantly needs repair. She can pre-pay funeral plans for herself and Joe since such plans are exempt assets for Medicaid purposes.

As she's fixing up the house she realizes that over the long run she might not be able to afford to remain there. After Joe has qualified for Medicaid, she thinks she might need to sell the house and move to an inexpensive apartment in a retirement community near the nursing home. Thus, she decides to spend whatever funds remain of the $54,100 "over resource" amount on making her home more attractive, and therefore more valuable, if and when she sells it. New carpet, new appliances, fresh paint and repair of the front porch would make her home much more saleable. Because all of those expenditures are improvements to an exempt asset – the home – the improvements themselves are exempt as part of that exempt home. She will be converting countable assets to exempt assets.

For purposes of Joe's eligibility for Medicaid, assume that Helen and Joe had previously executed reciprocal durable powers of attorney in which they authorized each other to transfer to themselves all assets of the spouse who becomes ill. That POA included express and unlimited spousal gifting powers as well as the specific authority to deal with each other's ownership interest in their home, which was specifically described in the power of attorney.

But what about a cash gift to Helen's and Joe's grandson? First of all, they did not make that gift for purposes of qualifying for Medicaid, so it should not be penalized. Unfortunately, however, all transfers for less than fair market value are presumed to be disqualifying gifts until proved to the contrary. In this case, however, there will be no gifting issue. Helen and Joe gave their grandson money six years ago. The look-back period for gifts is five years, thus placing the gift to grandson beyond the scrutiny of Medicaid.

IMPORTANT NOTE: The variations from one Medicaid case to another in terms of assets, income, costs, spending plans and family situations are infinite. Planning for Medicaid eligibility is extremely complex and must be done *exactly* right. The timing of each action taken by an applicant and his/her spouse can also control the outcome. The above, simplistic, example is for illustration only. Medicaid planning absolutely requires consultation with an experienced elder law attorney in your jurisdiction. The National Academy of Elder Law Attorneys provides an online data base listing by state of attorneys who can help with Medicaid applications. www.naela.org

HOUSING OPTIONS

There are many options for seniors for retirement living and, in the event of incapacity, long-term care. "Aging in Place" refers to remaining in your own home or moving to a home you purchase or rent in an elder-friendly environment. As discussed below, retirement living options include everything from a "Village Model" to traditional retirement communities (golf, happy hour and fun), to Assisted Living Facilities (ALFs), where most of your needs including social activities, are taken care of, to Nursing Homes (at home in a hospital-like setting). Continuing Care Retirement Communities (CCRCs) are also an important option to consider for those who can afford them, as they combine on one campus everything from independent living apartments to assisted living to nursing home level of care.

Note that the Fair Housing Act defines housing for seniors as an exempt category from discriminatory housing policies. Housing intended for, and solely occupied by, persons age 62 and older or housing in which at least 80% of the occupied units have at least one person who is 55 or older, may legally discriminate against younger applicants.

Aging at Home

Aging at home is preferred by most individuals. It offers a comfortable and familiar environment, feelings of independence and security, and familiarity and proximity to family and friends. If you already own your own home and/or you use a reverse mortgage to afford care (as discussed in a later section), living at home may be a less expensive option than moving to a retirement community or nursing home. If you rent or pay a mortgage, and you also need care services, it may cost more to stay at home versus living in a facility. Facilities can provide more than just a residence. They can also consolidate residents' care, meals and social activities. Trade-offs between staying in your own home and moving to a facility include reduction in personal privacy, the "feel" of being institutionalized, limitations on food choices, doing things on somebody else's schedule and so forth.

New technologies that can assist with long-distance monitoring of an elderly loved-one are available to give peace of mind to families as well. These can go far beyond the "nanny-cams" and emergency response necklaces most people are aware of. Current technology allows for more monitoring, or less intrusion, or other individualized options to help you remain as safely independent as possible in your own home.

Safety Proofing the Home

If both safety and financial considerations permit, you can take steps to help yourself remain at home, using caregivers and services in the community as needed. If you're planning to remain in your own home, you should consider having your home checked for safety. A Professional Geriatric Care Manager (GCM), also known as an Aging Life Care Expert™, can walk through your house noticing whether you are vulnerable to such things as hazardous loose rugs or other impediments, whether you can easily reach plugs and light switches, whether available devices would make it easier for you to care for your pet, and so forth. You might also want to consider outfitting your home with amenities and assistance devices in order to allow you to safely remain living there, such as a wheelchair ramp or staircase elevator. You might need to have your kitchen and bathroom sinks reconfigured to accommodate a wheel chair or motorized scooter. Companies and contractors that specialize in this field call themselves "Universal Design" or "Accessible Design" contractors and remodelers. Some of the remodeling work done to make living in your home easier and safer can be tax deductible. It is best to talk to your CPA before planning your universal design home modifications.

Meals on Wheels (MOW)

Local Meals on Wheels (MOW) programs usually offer two meals a day on weekdays delivered to homebound elderly individuals who are unable to shop and cook for themselves. Some MOW programs provide meals seven days a week. The cost varies by locale. Some Meals on Wheels programs even provide Meals for Pets, which enables clients to keep their independence and their beloved dog or cat. Financial assistance may be available. You can locate your local provider at www.mowaa.org or by calling the Meals on Wheels Association of America at 1-888-998-6325.

Durable Medical Equipment (DME)

In addition to outfitting your home to make it easier and safer to live there with disabilities, residents may be able to benefit from Durable Medical Equipment (DME). Many items such as wheelchairs, oxygen tanks, lifts, hospital beds, toileting and shower assistive devices and grab bars, to name a few, can be delivered to your home. DME is often covered by Medicare as long as the patient has a Certificate of Medical Necessity (CMN) or a Written Confirmation of Verbal Order (WCVO) from a physician. The equipment rental is covered at 80% by Medicare for a period of about a year. Medigap policies will likely make up the remaining 20% cost. The patient will be given an option of purchasing the equipment as the rental deadline approaches.

Items such as an elevator are not considered medical necessities and are not covered by Medicare, but they may be tax deductible. Check with your tax advisor. Your tax advisor can also advise you about the required physician paperwork needed to claim the deduction.

You may obtain information about finding companies that supply Durable Medical Equipment by searching that term online, or contacting your local Area Agency on Aging (AAA). Some Area Agencies on Aging have different names in different jurisdictions. To find one in your area, do a Google-type search on "Area Agency on Aging and Your City and State."

Taking Away the Keys

Those who are aging in place are usually accustomed to the independence and convenience of driving themselves wherever they need to go. It is not uncommon, however, that the vicissitudes of aging can sneak up on them. Their visual acuity declines; their reflexes slow; their hearing no longer alerts them to sirens. For many, the day eventually comes when they can no longer drive without endangering the safety of themselves or others. Suggestions to elderly persons that they can no longer drive safely are often met with vehement resistance and insistence that they can still drive as well as ever.

The best way for you and your elderly loved-one to determine whether they should still be driving is for them to voluntarily take a written and physical driving test. If your elderly loved-one is so sure they are OK to drive, kindly ask them to take the tests so that everyone concerned can "get off their back." They will hopefully agree in order to prove their point. If they do not agree, even with the request of people who really care about them, then it is a sign they should perhaps not be driving.

If you do have to threaten to "take away the keys," be prepared for your loved one to be angry and defensive. If feasible, however, you can try to transfer this decision to a neutral third party. If you are a family member concerned about your loved-one continuing to drive despite the possible risk to themselves and others, you may be able to report him or her to the Department of Motor Vehicles (DMV), depending on your locality. In this case, the DMV might invite (or summon) your loved one to come in to take a routine vision and driving test. The DMV may also conduct an interview and require passing of both a written and driving test. If your loved one's license is revoked, it wasn't revoked by you.

Some physicians are willing to participate in the process by writing a letter recommending that the patient stop driving. However, physicians are increasingly reluctant to become involved in such sensitive matters and are also concerned about physician-patient confidentiality issues.

Many states require a vision exam or a written statement from an eye doctor for drivers beginning at various ages between 62-85 depending on the state, and some states change the length of time required between license renewals at certain ages.

Family members' realization that their loved ones can no longer drive causes trauma to all concerned. After getting past the perceived "attack" on the elderly person's capabilities, there is also the practical question of how the new non-driver is going to get around. For elderly persons residing with a loved one, such as an adult child, the trauma of losing the car keys can be minimized. It is important to be able to propose a plan ahead of time as to how getting around will still happen for them. For those without a live-in chauffeur, see the discussion below.

Getting There After the Car Keys Are Gone

So now you (or your loved one) find yourself stuck at home. How will you buy groceries? Pick up prescriptions? Visit the mall? Get to the doctor's office?

Transportation issues constitute probably the single most important worry faced by those who want to age at home but can no longer drive their own cars. The loss of independence is profound after a lifetime of being able to come and go wherever and whenever you pleased. You can no longer hop in your car for a trip to the supermarket, to doctors' appointments, to hair appointments and even to your favorite deli. If you do not drive, there are a few options to consider.

In many areas, cities or counties offer free van services which will pick you – and others – up at your door and take you where you need to go. To qualify for this free service, individuals must have a disability defined by the Americans with Disabilities Act and, as a result, be unable to utilize fixed-route transportation such as metro bus and Metrorail. You can also qualify if you need to use a ramp or wheelchair lift to board or exit a public transit vehicle but no such acceptable public transit vehicle is being operated at the time, date, and route you would travel. Or you must be unable to travel from a bus stop or rail station to and from your destinations. These vans serve several people at a time, so direct non-stop service to where you want to go is unlikely.

The obvious advantage of the city-county provided transportation services is that, like volunteers, their services are free or low cost. A problem with these services is that they are relatively inflexible in terms of both pick-up times and destinations. Many communities have volunteer resources through religious and not-for-profit groups that offer free or low-cost rides for elderly. Certain cab companies offer discounts and specially trained drivers whose vehicles have wheelchair ramps (not lifts).

You can buy or rent a wheelchair van. Rentals with drivers cost about $80 to $140 per hour depending on where you live. Purchasing a wheelchair van can cost anywhere from $5000 to $60,000. Friends, family and sometimes home health aides (depending on their company's rules) can drive the van for you.

Concierge companion services provide another option, tantamount to having your own personal chauffeur. These companions will take you wherever you want to go when you want to go, just as if you were getting into your own car and driving yourself. They will take you to your doctor's office and even sit in with you if you wish them to take notes. They will take you to your hair appointment. They will take you and your pet to the vet or the groomer. Like you, if you were driving yourself, they will make stops so you can buy a birthday gift for your niece, visit your favorite deli, and fill your prescriptions, while providing educated, warm companionship along the way.

Concierge companion services, such as those of the company I founded in 2005, are an excellent solution for many clients. Such private companies charge from about $30 to $70 per hour. They are not limited merely to providing driving services; many provide services from grocery shopping to locating pet walkers and house cleaners for you, to locating and supervising handymen, plumbers and electricians for home maintenance needs, and, for many, sociable companion services to accompany you on your walks around the block or to the movies for example.

AAA estimates that driving a typical car an average distance per year costs the driver-owner about $8,558 per year. Older individuals tend to use their cars less frequently and over shorter distances, so let's reduce that average to $6000 per year. At $50 per hour for driving and companion services by a private concierge, two hours of private driving, errand running, and companionship per week for one year would cost only $5200 per year. With concierge drivers, you have your own chauffeur and companion for likely just a little more than it cost you when you could still drive yourself in your own car.

Senior Centers

Seniors living at home may experience loneliness or might require some care during the day. For reasonably healthy elders, participating in the activities of a Senior Center, often located within local community centers, can be a welcome respite from the four walls of their homes. A Senior Center is a community center geared toward seniors. It provides opportunities for seniors who are retired and looking for stimulation to socialize, take classes and participate in field trips. Fees for Senior Centers are usually very low, if any. Senior Centers can be located through local Area Agency on Aging programs.

Adult Day Care Centers

For those who can benefit from activities and companionship, but who need some care and supervision, adult day care centers offer a solution. Adult day care has the additional benefit of giving the primary caregiver at home some much appreciated time to themselves, or time for their own employment needs.

Adult day care centers are non-residential facilities specializing in providing activities for elderly and physically disabled individuals. Most centers operate 10 to 12 hours per day providing meals, social or recreational outings, and general supervision. Adult day care centers operate either under a social model or a healthcare model. Healthcare model centers may focus on providing care only for individuals with Alzheimer's Disease and related dementias. Some day care centers maintain a nurse on site. Occasionally, there will be a small room dedicated to the checking of participants' vital signs by nurses or medical technicians. Some centers may also provide transportation and personal care as well as counseling for caregivers.

There are approximately 5,685 adult day care centers operating in the United States providing care for about 321,000 older Americans each day. The average cost is approximately $68 per day and meals are included. For families caring for dementia patients, adult day care centers provide family-strengthening respite to the primary caregivers.

To locate an adult day care center, senior center, transportation information and more, search the Eldercare Locator at http://www.eldercare.gov.

The Village Model

The Village Model is an aging-at-home option which is rapidly growing in popularity. These communities are also called Naturally Occurring Retirement Communities (NORC). They are generally located in a city landscape where neighborhoods or designated groups of residential blocks are defined as being part of The Village.

In some types of Village Models, elderly residents pay a fee to support a database and administrative costs such as a phone line to a concierge person with trusted resources for the community. The concierge contact will also maintain a list of residents who are willing to volunteer their services, both skilled and unskilled, to other neighbors within The Village.

Maintaining access to free services through neighbors and a trusted list of professional providers supports the goal of the Village Model which is to allow residents to age in place and not have to move to an assisted living facility.

Some Village Models are highly organized and use website technology to communicate their services to the residents. This model often charges hefty annual dues to maintain this high level of service. Alternatively, some Villages are loosely maintained and use sign-up sheets and phone tree lists to communicate to residents how they can obtain help from neighbors. Typically, this model charges no fee, or nominal fees, to its residents for participation. You can find more information at www.vtvnetwork.org.

Another new concept similar to the Village Model is the **Greenhouse Model**, covered below in the Long-Term Care Nursing Home section of this book below.

Selling and Moving from Your Home

If and when the time comes that you need to move out of your home in exchange for a facility which can provide more services, you will confront layers of issues not found in other moving situations. The National Association of Realtors has a specific designation for specially trained realtors for older adults. They are called Senior Real Estate Specialists (SRES). Through special training and education, they have advanced knowledge of how to best approach the unique facets of listing, selling and relocating for those who are over 50. Sometimes the benefits are obvious, such as having a realtor who can come to the home to obtain signatures in an era when electronic signatures and emails are the expected norm. Less obvious help can come through the understanding that although keeping the gold velvet flocked wallpaper may require a lower asking price, there is a trade-off. The realtor should be sensitive in considering how to discuss ripping down that beloved 50-year old wallpaper. Individuals who think they might benefit from a SRES realtor in the selling and moving process can locate a Senior Real Estate Specialist at this website: www.seniorsrealestate.com

Companion and Concierge services in your community can also assist you through the physical and emotional hurdles of the move itself. They can help you sort through the things you have accumulated over a lifetime and assist you to make the tough decisions between "keep," "donate" and "toss." They can arrange for an estate sale for you. When you arrive at your new home, they can help you arrange your furniture, unpack your moving boxes and even hang your pictures and put away your dishes.

RESIDENTIAL ALTERNATIVES

Independent/Active Adult/Retirement Communities

Active Adult Communities were originally referred to as "retirement communities." These communities have special facilities catering to the needs of recent retirees, including extensive amenities like clubhouses, swimming pools, arts and crafts, boating, golf courses, and retail. Active Adult Communities have significantly dwindled in numbers. It can be difficult to uproot and move when this environment can no longer provide for the care needs of a resident whose health is in decline. This realization has led to the growth of Continuing Care Retirement Communities (CCRCs) discussed below.

Independent living options may be stand-alone or may be combined in the same building or campus with Assisted Living level care.

Assisted Living Facilities (ALFs)

Assisted Living Facilities (ALFs) generally come in two forms: large traditional facilities which average 40 to 100 units and small assisted living facilities which average 3 to 10 units. Many ALFs provide supervision for dementia patients who can wander and forget to take care of themselves. Unlike nursing homes, most ALFs offer private rooms, some with kitchenettes. Residents have meals in the dining room, aides to help them dress and bathe, and they participate in organized activities and outings. Some ALFs offer a visiting doctor to see residents on-site; others obtain medical care off site and get there either via family/friends driving them, a companion company driving them or a van provided by the ALF. Monthly costs for assisted living facilities vary greatly across the country. A very general range is $2,000 to $10,000 per month depending on location, private rooms, etc. The national average is currently calculated to be $3,600.

Small Assisted Living Facilities are usually located in private homes with a small group of people. The bedrooms are real bedrooms, and the kitchen and dining spaces are much smaller than a cafeteria-like large occupancy facility. They tend to be less expensive than large assisted living facilities; however, they often do not provide the constant activities and entertainment provided by larger facilities. Some people prefer the quieter atmosphere of the small assisted living facilities.

Large Assisted Living Facilities may offer both private and non-private rooms or apartments. There is usually no special medical monitoring equipment except for emergency call bells, and skilled nursing staff may not be available at all hours. As is the case with small ALFs, household chores are performed by staff, and meals are cooked and served on site. Some facilities have beauty salons and/or religious services on the premises. Many have limited van transport to grocery stores and a medical complex for residents' doctor appointments on certain days of the week. They offer a variety of activities for residents such as exercise classes, live music performances, field trips and book discussions.

Some facilities allow pets and some have resident "pets," a cat or dog that lives among the residents to add to the feeling of being at "home." Most residents are free to come and go, restrained only by any limiting physical conditions or limited transportation provided by the facility. Additionally, residents with moderate or severe dementia who are in danger of becoming disoriented, may need to be accompanied when they are out of the facility. ALFs offer visiting nurses, doctors and podiatrists. Other ALFs might provide a van to take residents to appointments and shopping. When that is not an option, residents rely on family, friends or paid companion services for transportation.

Typically, an assisted living resident needs assistance with an average of two or three Activities of Daily Living (ADLs). Most residents initially move in when they need help with two ADLs.

Activities of Daily Living are:

- personal hygiene (bathing) and grooming,
- dressing and undressing,
- self-feeding,
- transferring (getting in and out of a bed or wheelchair),
- toileting and/or continence care, and
- ambulation (walking without an assistive device).

If the level of care needed eventually exceeds what can be provided in an ALF, a resident will have to move to a facility offering a higher level of care, such as a nursing home. It is wise to inquire ahead of time what a facility considers to be a "cut-off" point. For example, some will not allow residents who develop dementia to remain in the residence. Others have designated floors or units especially for dementia residents that will only require a move to a different section of the facility.

Long-Term Care Nursing Homes

Long-term care nursing homes provide patients with a residence in a hospital-like setting. They should not be confused with skilled nursing facilities (SNFs,) that provide post-hospital skilled and rehabilitation care and are covered by Medicare.

Long-term care is the type of care needed by Alzheimer's patients and those with other dementing or extremely disabling conditions, such as damage from a severe stroke. These facilities care for the most ill and disabled seniors. They look like hospitals in that residents have a hospital bed, a dresser and a TV, usually in a room shared with another person. Residents who live in nursing homes receive on-site access to medical doctors, skilled nurses, nurse's aides and various types of therapists. Most long-term nursing home care is provided by Certified Nursing Assistants (CNAs) – not by skilled personnel. This means that only about 5% of the care received in such nursing homes qualifies as "skilled medical care" and is covered by Medicare or Medigap policies. The remaining 95% of costs must be privately paid out-of-pocket, or with the assistance of long-term care insurance, or, ultimately, by Medicaid. Medicaid may pay for the entire cost of a nursing home depending on each state's financial qualifications.

The average annual cost of private pay in a long-term care facility has risen to about $82,000 for a semi-private room. Private rooms cost about $92,300. Medicaid for long-term care currently pays approximately half of that cost in this country. Long-term care insurance, for those who bought policies while they were still healthy enough to qualify, also covers a substantial amount of the cost.

A nursing home cannot "require" a third party (such as an adult child) to sign an agreement saying they are the "responsible party." Read all admission forms carefully.

The difference between a skilled nursing facility (a.k.a. nursing home,) and an assisted living facility, is that in a nursing home, skilled medical can be provided regularly. For a resident who needs an IV, or feeding tube and constant monitoring for transferring, or help being fed, a nursing home can provide these services regularly. Some assisted living facilities can provide some of these things intermittently.

Green Houses

Just like there are "small assisted living facilities" mentioned above, there are also "small nursing homes" and their popularity is on the rise. A green house is a cluster of apartments or rooms within a home that have skilled nursing services like a large nursing home. However, unlike large nursing homes, they look a lot less like a hospital. There is a shared kitchen, shared activity rooms and the high level of support offered by skilled medical professionals. Like a nursing home, Green Houses can accept Medicare for part of the services and Medicaid, possibly to cover all of the cost. For more information see: http://thegreenhouseproject.org.

The Centers for Medicare and Medicaid Services (CMS) has a website, which allows users to see how well facilities perform using a five-star rating program, compare nursing home on www.medicare.gov.

Continuing Care Retirement Communities (CCRCs)

Continuing Care Retirement Communities (CCRCs) are also known as "life care communities." This is a newer type of retirement community where a spectrum of aging care needs can be met in one location. CCRCs offer independent living apartments, assisted living facilities and on-site nursing homes. If an independent living resident requires additional care, the CCRC will provide that care in the resident's apartment for as long as possible. As the need for care increases, the resident will move to one of the assisted living units. In a worst case, residents who develop illnesses such as Alzheimer's Disease will be moved to the CCRC's nursing home.

Typically, elderly candidates move into a CCRC while still living independently, with few health risks or health care needs, and continue to reside there independently until the end of life. Many CCRCs require a resident to move in at the stage of life where they are generally free of illness or disability. Residents benefit from knowing they will never be required to move from the campus, and for couples who age at different rates, spouses can be "near" each other, even if their residential care needs differ.

Generally, residences in CCRCs are not owned. Although many people think of CCRC apartments as condominiums, they are not actually real property owned by the resident. What people buy is a "care contract," assuring them of care throughout the rest of their lives. Some CCRCs charge entrance fees in the hundreds of thousands of dollars and have varying contracts for monthly fees or fees based on care needs thereafter.

CCRCs advertise that they re-invest collected fees, hoping to add worth until the resident requires more expensive care. As residents advance in age and their medical needs change, the level of care and services increases proportionally. The needs of the residents are consistently monitored and catered to, particularly as those needs become more demanding. If greater illness or injury warrants hospitalization, the resident may return to the CCRC after recovery. Indeed, most CCRCs have on-site rehab centers to assist with the transition from hospital to residence.

It is important to note that if a resident needs one-on-one care from a CNA or health aide regularly, and wants to remain in their unit and not the assisted living or nursing section of the CCRC, they may have to pay out of pocket for those services – they are usually not covered in the down payment or monthly fee.

In recent years, some CCRCs have made front page news when communities "ran out" of the up-front money that was meant to ensure the "money would always be there." Some CCRCs are now structuring things differently and do not require large down payments. Because of the long-term obligations and large sums of money involved with CCRCs, many local Area Agencies on Aging have information and tip sheets on their websites to help clarify the options.

PROFESSIONAL CAREGIVERS: WHO DOES WHAT

There are many different types of professionals available to help with healthcare needs in many different settings such as home, assisted living, nursing facilities, and hospice care, either in the patient's home or a hospice facility. Elder care professionals include: Professional Geriatric Care Managers/AKA Aging Life Care Managers TM (GCM), Geriatrician M.D.s, Social Workers, Registered Nurses (RN), Licensed Practical Nurses (LPN), Home Health/Nurse Aides, Therapists (physical, occupational, speech, psychologists, dieticians), and lastly but also important, non-healthcare companions. Some companies provide several of these professionals through a single company, and some only provide one. A growing trend is the "all in one" home health company, providing a visiting doctor, skilled help (like physical therapy, RN visits for needs like catheter changes) and Certified Nursing Assistants (CNA) who help with personal care.

Geriatric Care Manager (GCM) a.k.a. Aging Life Care Expert™

Aging Life Care Managers (formerly called Geriatric Care Managers and hence the commonly recognized acronym has seemed to stick - GCMs) are degreed, licensed and certified specialists who assist seniors and disabled individuals and their families in handling crisis and meeting long-term care needs. Most professional Aging Life Care Managers have training in gerontology, social work, nursing, counseling, or elder law. Aging Life Care Managers have extensive experience in identifying problems and offering cost-effective solutions based on an individual's level of functioning and health, emotional well-being, finances, and legal documents.

GCMs can be vitally important to family members who are caring from a distance. In addition to being able to navigate home care options, assisted living, hospitalization, rehab, and nursing home issues, they are able to submit the kind of paperwork that allows for coverage by insurance, benefit programs, and government assistance. Aging Life Care management companies usually charge between $100 and $200 per hour for geriatric care management work. They are not covered by Medicaid, Medicare, or by most medical insurance policies. However, clients may be able to bill some services to long-term care insurance, depending on the history of the individual case. Such services might also be tax deductible as medical expenses. The internet link www.aginglifecare.org has more information.

Example:

An 87-year-old woman had fallen, broken her hip, undergone surgery at the hospital and was discharged to a local Skilled Nursing Facility (SNF) for short-term rehab. Her only daughter was living a plane-ride away, and felt she could not manage her mother's care the way she wanted from afar. She hired an Aging Life Care Manager to oversee that her mother's needs were being met at the SNF, advocate if needed, and communicate with her on a regular basis about how her mother was doing.

Geriatrician

Geriatricians are physicians who specialize in the care of elderly people or those older adults who are presenting with diseases and disabilities characteristic of the elderly. Doctors who make this their specialty are listed in medical directories under the category of Geriatrics.

A physician who does not specialize in working with older adults had an 80-year-old male in his office who just moved across the country to be in an Assisted Living Facility (ALF) closer to his children. This was his first visit with his physician, and he was having irregular bowels. The physician said he should start taking fiber supplements and sent him on his way. The 80-year-old male's son brought him back to the ALF with MetaFiber that they bought at the drug store. When he and his father gave it to the nurse at the ALF she asked for the doctor's order. Unfortunately, they and the physician did not realize that it is standard protocol at Assisted Living and Skilled Nursing Facilities to have a prescription for any new or previously discontinued medication or supplement for that resident. A geriatrician would have known this and provided the man and his son with what they needed. Geriatricians are very familiar with "co-morbid" conditions because many elders have a variety of common age-related issues all at once. Cross-referencing all of the conditions is par for the course.

Registered Nurse (RN)

Registered Nurses generally have about four years of professional education and often supervise tasks performed by Licensed Practical Nurses (LPNs), orderlies, and nursing assistants. They can also administer most medications, including intravenous (IV) push-meds, take blood pressure and other measurements, and perform related tasks. Registered Nurses are covered by Medicare while you are in a facility or for short periods of time under Medicare In-Home Coverage, Hospice coverage or long-term care insurances plans. Companies that provide them charge about $75-$125 per visit private pay if the service does not qualify for insurance coverage.

Example:

A woman living in the Independent Living section of a Continuing Care Retirement Community, had a minor fall in her apartment but was able to stand up on her own. About a half hour later she realized she was bleeding on her elbow. She went to the RN at the Wellness Clinic in her community and the RN was able to clean the wound, and bandage it. The RN assessed the wound and did not feel it needed the attention of the ER. If she has then needed wound care- which is considered a skilled treatment, the RN would have been able to handle that for her.

Licensed Practical Nurse (LPN)

Licensed Practical Nurses (LPNS) usually have two years of professional training and can administer most medications and IVs (except push IVs which administer medications intravenously), take blood pressure and other measurements, and perform related tasks.

Although RNs and LPNs generally cost the same private pay on a per-visit basis through an agency that provides skilled nursing, if you are interested in hiring a private nurse for longer periods of time to be in your home because you need frequent medications or IVs, an LPN generally charges less than an RN, about $40 an hour. Please note, as discussed below, a Home Health Aide (HHA)/Certified Nursing Assistant (CNA) may not administer any medications but may simply direct a patient to take medications from a pre-sorted pill dispenser.

Example:

An LPN at an Assisted Living Facility was administering a new medication to a resident a few days after the medication was started. The resident was complaining of loose stools, and the LPN knew that this was a possible side effect from the new medication the resident started. She contacted the physician to inform them and ask what they would like her to have the resident do. The physician decreased the dose of the medication over the phone and the LPN advised the resident and family member of the change.

The below-mentioned therapists may be covered under regular health insurance, or may be covered by The Medicare Part A In-Home Care Program or for limited periods of time following discharge from a hospital or rehab facility.

Social Worker (MSW or LCSW)

Social workers may have a BSW or an MSW (bachelor's and master's in social work respectively.) Licensed Social Workers (LSWs) and Licensed Clinical Social Workers

(LCSWs) have a different level of licensure, and depending on the state, they can practice privately without supervision. LSWs typically practice within an agency or facility setting with supervision. All social workers are licensed by their individual states. Some of their services may be covered by Medicare and Medicaid.

LCSWs usually work within the context of a government agency such as Departments of Health and Human Services which assist low income individuals with Medicaid applications or finding care resources. They also work in the care management field because they are knowledgeable in counseling and in financial issues surrounding qualification for benefits. Social Workers also prepare discharge plans for patients leaving medical or rehab facilities. They are employed by such facilities to provide support and information to a patient and a family during the stay and, most importantly, in the transition from the facility back into the community. They can also play an important support role for patients and families going through hospice care.

Example:

A 92-year-old man was found by his neighbors wandering in the neighborhood one evening asking where he lived. The neighbors contacted 911 and he was brought to the hospital. After a few days in the hospital, tests showed that the man had a urinary tract infection and a bad respiratory infection. He did not have any children. The social worker at the hospital discussed with him the importance of going to a Skilled Nursing Facility (SNF) until he was fully recovered. He agreed, even though he was reluctant to not return to his home right away. The social worker found him a facility and coordinated the discharge from the hospital and admission to the SNF.

Physical Therapist (PT)

Physical Therapists generally assist with restoring function, restoring mobility, and relieving pain.

Occupational Therapist (OT)

Occupational Therapists generally assist with improving the ability to perform tasks of daily living, such as tasks impaired by brain injuries and memory issues. For example, they would provide training on list-making to aid recall, or retraining an individual on performing simple tasks of daily living.

Speech Therapist (ST)

Speech Therapists assist with voice and communication disorders and, importantly, swallowing issues which are especially problematic for stroke victims and late stage Alzheimer's patients.

Example:

A 92-year-old man's daughter brought him out to dinner, for their weekly visit. She noticed that he was coughing during the entire meal. When she brought him back to the Skilled Nursing Facility where he lived, she reported the coughing to the nurse. The nurse stated she would call his physician. The physician and nurse decided the man could be losing his ability to swallow safely, so the physician ordered a Speech (ST) to perform an assessment to see if he is aspirating (inhaling) his food. When someone aspirates the food goes down into the lungs and causes them to cough and possibly develop aspiration pneumonia, a life-threatening condition. An ST can help them relearn how to eat, or suggest they start eating a modified diet of ground or pureed food.

Note: PT, OT and Speech therapies are offered in facilities, or in private homes.

Home Health Aide (HHA), Certified Nursing Assistant (CNA) and Personal Care Assistant (PCA)

Health aides undergo a short training period - a few weeks - for their certification. In a home setting, they are typically called Home Health Aides (HHAs) or Personal Care Assistant (PCAs). When they are in an institutional setting they are called Certified Nursing Assistants (CNAs). They typically have similar training and perform the same duties - oftentimes the titles are used interchangeably. HHAs, CNAs and PCAs assist with "personal care" needs such as dressing, bathing, feeding, toileting and transferring. As mentioned, they cannot administer medications from a pill bottle, but may only offer medications via a pre-sorted pill dispenser.

Aides are generally available for hire in 4 to 24-hour live-in shifts. The companies that provide them usually charge approximately $15 to $30 per hour for their services, depending on where you live. If you hire an aide to live-in, there is usually a bulk-rate cost, because you are generally not paying for the time during which they are sleeping.

Patients needing care and attention at night may require two aides in 12-hour shifts for which the hourly rate could be charged for the 24-hour period.

Medicare only covers a few hours a week of help from an aide if you qualify for short term Medicare In-Home coverage. Consequently, if you do not qualify for Medicare In-Home and do not have long-term care insurance, the cost to you for a four-hour per day shift (based on an average round number of $20 per hour) will be $560 per week, for an eight-hour shift it will be $1120 per week etc. The cost for a typical live-in could be around $1,750 depending on where you live per week. A good long-term care insurance policy as discussed below can cover much of this out-of-pocket cost.

Each jurisdiction has its own rules governing issues such as training and background checks for direct-care workers. Generally speaking, in order to be certified, HHAs, CNAs and PCAs, in addition to passing their certification tests, must pass a criminal background check and have a recent negative test result for tuberculosis. HHAs and PCAs are not usually required to have a high school diploma or G.E.D whereas, CNAs must in order to be admitted to any accredited program. These aides can assist with everyday activities such as bathing and often perform light housekeeping and cooking chores.

Example:

A 78-year-old woman living in her home tripped on a box on the floor, fell, and broke her arm. She was able to return home but needed some outpatient services. She had a CNA come in daily in the morning to help her get dressed for the day and assist her with any chores she needed to get completed. In the evenings, her daughter came by after work to help her get ready for bed. Once her arm was starting to heal she received PT at a local outpatient rehabilitation center to help her build the strength back in her arm. OT was then started to help her return to her prior level of functioning. OT was able to support her in learning how to safely use her arm until her range of motion returned and it fully healed.

Psychologist

Psychologists can assist with coping with the new challenges and changes of an illness or debilitating disease, not only for the patients, but also for their families.

Example:

A 78-year-old woman who lost her daughter to cancer was struggling with depression. She really needed to talk with someone about the loss. She was talking with her priest, but didn't feel he understood her perspective as a mother. Her priest suggested she reach out to a female psychologist, which the woman did. The psychologist helped her during her grieving process.

Neurologist

A neurologist is a medical doctor who treats disorders that affect the brain, spinal cord, and nerves, such as: Dementia, Cerebrovascular disease, such as stroke, Demyelinating diseases of the central nervous system, such as multiple sclerosis and Parkinson's Disease.

Elders are especially susceptible to such diseases and conditions.

Example:

A 75-year-old man told his doctor that he was having a hard time keeping track of appointments, medications, and even the names of his children. He was afraid that he had Alzheimer's Disease. He wanted to know what was going on and hopefully take a medication to help the memory impairment. His doctor referred him to a neurologist for a thorough evaluation. The neurologist administered multiple assessments and wrote a detailed summary of his findings. The man had a diagnosis of Vascular Dementia and by knowing this, he, his doctor, and children, were able to learn about the diagnosis, what preventative measures he could take and what would likely happen as it progressed.

Dietitian

Dietitians can assist in a variety of ways from analyzing nutritional needs, such as for diabetes patients, to creating shopping lists and food preparation instructions. They can cost up to about $125 per visit. Some nutrition services, particularly for diabetes and renal failure, may be covered by Medicare.

Example:

An Aging Life Care Manager took a client to a physician for a follow up regarding her new diagnosis of diabetes. The woman was used to eating a certain way her whole life and was having a hard time following the appropriate diet. Her physician instructed the Aging Life Care Manager and the patient to speak with the dietician at the Assisted Living Facility. The two of them met with the dietician and the dietician and client set up a good menu that was realistic for the woman, but also followed her physician's recommendations. The Aging Life Care Manager helped her succeed with this plan by talking with the staff at the Assisted Living Facility so they too would help her with her plan.

Companion

Non-health care companions vary significantly in training and background. They may be assigned by their company for a non-hands-on placement (typically to provide supervision care to patients who have dementia). These companions usually cost about $20 per hour and have a four-hour minimum. There are also companies or individuals who offer companion services privately in the $20 to $40 per hour price range. Often these are college graduates who advertise themselves as providing companion, concierge and transportation services. There is usually a two-hour minimum.

At the top of the companion price range, at $50 or more per hour, are companies that provide college-educated or retired professionals who provide companion services with a one hour minimum. These companions can stand in as an adult child for intellectual stimulation, bill paying, transportation to medical appointments, errands, and social outings. The variables in price range depend on whether you are buying bulk hours, as well as the education level of the companion. Another distinction is that, frequently, companions who are HHAs in the $20 per hour range do not drive and often take public transportation to get to the patient's home. Therefore, they cannot assist with errands and doctor appointments.

Example:

A 90-year-old woman was recently widowed after her husband of 70 years died from a heart attack. She was alone in her house and her children lived far away. The woman was functioning independently, and had a family friend that would take her to her doctor appointments. However, she was very anxious about living alone and sad that she had no one to talk to or cook for. Her children hired a companion for her that simply spent time talking with her, had lunch with her, and was there for her a few hours a day to help her adjust to this loss.

Note: fees vary depending on locality, with metro regions demanding higher per-hour charges for these services than rural areas, and the more rural the area, the less likely it is that you would find these services available at all.

SOCIAL SECURITY

Social Security Overview

President Franklin Roosevelt signed the Social Security Act into law in 1935 and stated that it was meant to provide "some measure of protection…against the loss of a job and against poverty-ridden old age." The Act provided Social Security benefits to retired workers when they reached age 65. Life expectancy in 1930 was 58 for men and 62 for women. Therefore, Social Security income was originally intended for those *really old* folks who made it past age 65. In 2010, the life expectancy was 75.7 for men and 80.8 for women. In 1961, President John F. Kennedy added an early retirement option for individuals age 62.

The Social Security Administration (SSA) invests only in government-issued or government-guaranteed securities. Government securities often grow at a slower rate than other types of investments.

The amount of Social Security you receive is based on the employment taxes you and your employer paid into the system during your working years. It is the major source of income for *most* seniors. Nine out of ten seniors receive Social Security. For one in five seniors, Social Security payments constitute almost their entire income. Social Security raises approximately one in three seniors out of poverty.

The Social Security Administration is a federal agency that provides various programs related to retirement, disability, and dependent/survivor benefits. The technical name for these benefits is Old Age, Survivors and Disability Insurance (OASDI).

Social Security Benefits

There are different types of Social Security insurance benefits.

To understand these benefits, please note the following definitions: A *Primary Worker* is the individual whose work record qualifies him or her, as well as certain family members, to receive Social Security benefits. The *Primary Insurance Amount (PIA)* is the benefit amount a Primary Worker is eligible to receive at his or her full retirement age.

Overview:
Social Security is a retirement benefit you receive because as a Primary Worker you and your employer paid payroll taxes into the program during your working years. You may enroll any time after the age of 62 and receive a monthly payment.

Dependent's and Survivor's Benefits are benefits that can be received by people who qualify as dependents of a Primary Worker or survivors of a Primary Worker, such as a spouse, dependent or disabled child.

Social Security Disability Insurance (SSDI) is for people who have paid into Social Security and are both disabled and earning less *from working* than a threshold amount (so even a millionaire with lots of dividends can qualify). Certain people with disabilities can also qualify for SSDI based on the PIA of a retired, disabled or deceased parent.

Supplemental Security Income (SSI) is technically not a Social Security program although it is administered by the Social Security Administration (SSA). SSI is actually a welfare program that provides extra income to those who are 65 or older or are younger than 65 but are blind or have certain disabilities, and who fall below a certain poverty level of income *and* assets (about $2000).

The *Primary Insurance Amount* (PIA) is based on three things: *credits*, showing that you worked "enough" to receive a benefit amount, *income* you earned in dollar amounts per year and, the *number of years* you worked.

Employee Retirement and Disability Benefits

The Social Security *Primary Insurance Amount* (PIA) is not insurance like medical insurance, payable according to medical care you received. It actually combines both retirement and life insurance characteristics. It provides a monthly income benefit while you are still alive, and it acts like life insurance in that it makes payments to qualifying family members after you die.

Work Credits

In the past, Social Security calculated your benefits based on how many "quarters" in a year you earned income from working. A worker needed to earn 40 quarters of work totaling 10 years. In 1978, the term "quarters" changed to "credits." Instead of earning quarters based on set periods of time worked, workers began earning credits based on dollar amounts earned annually. This was especially helpful for people who worked seasonally and didn't necessarily work for all quarters of the year. Each year a dollar amount is set for which an individual can earn a credit. In 2017, an individual can earn one credit for each $1,300 of earnings up to four credits a year.

Payroll Tax

Generally, a payroll tax rate of 15.3% of gross income is shared by the employer and the employee; each pays half, which is 7.65%. This amount, if further broken down, is 6.2% for

Social Security up to a gross annual income amount of $127,200 (in 2017) and 1.45% for Medicare on all gross income, even that above the Social Security maximum. Self-employed workers must pay into Social Security of their own accord, through self-employment taxes, since they do not have taxes withheld from their pay. If you are self-employed, you or your accountant must be sure to pay the self-employment tax rate of 15.3% in quarterly federal estimated taxes.

During the year 2011, the *Tax Relief, Unemployment Insurance Reauthorization and Job Creation Act of 2010* lowered the amount that employees pay from 6.2% to 4.2%, and the self-employment rate from 12.4% to 10.4% for the Social Security element of the self-employment tax. The percentages have since returned to the standard as of 2013.

Also as of 2013, an additional 0.9% Medicare tax applies to individuals earning $200,000 and couples earning $250,000 and above.

Calculations

The SSA calculates a worker's Primary Insurance Amount (PIA) based on his or her highest 35 years of earnings. For those who worked fewer than 35 years, the years not worked are then added in as zeros. Earning fewer than 40 credits affects whether a worker will eventually have a co-pay for Medicare Part A (discussed in a previous chapter). Having fewer than 40 credits can also affect disability and survivor benefit amounts.

Most people have been accustomed to receiving a Social Security Benefit Statement every year, about three months before their birthday. To cut costs, these mailings have been mostly discontinued. The discontinuation of mailed statements for older people has been so controversial that the Administrator of SSA recently told the Congress that mailed statements to individuals over age 60 will be resumed.

The Social Security Administration has a "Retirement Estimator" tool on the www.ssa.gov website. The online tool will generally work if you have earned 40 credits, but there are some case-by-case exceptions whereby you will not be able to get your estimate.

An individual may apply for benefits 90 days prior to retirement by calling 1-800-772-1213 or logging on to the online services section of the Social Security website. www.ssa.gov. Be prepared to provide supportive documentation of citizenship and work records if asked. If these methods are not successful, you should make an appointment with your local Social Security office and state that your matter is "urgent" because a delay in applying can mean a delay in benefits.

Monthly Income

Currently, the average amount of Social Security retirement income is about $1,360 per month.

Social Security payments are usually made by direct deposit to your bank account and cover the prior month. For those who do not have a bank account, benefit payments can be loaded onto a Direct Express® Debit Card. Paper checks are being phased out altogether and anyone applying for Social Security after May of 2011 will no longer be able to opt for a paper check. Direct deposits are beneficial in several ways, perhaps the most important being that payment can be received by beneficiaries in a way that does not expose them to check thieves. Direct deposits also allow time to report a death to the SSA, which has the cost-effective result of the SSA having to retrieve fewer payments from accounts of deceased beneficiaries. Recipients are not entitled to any payment for the month in which they die, not even for the portion of the month they were living.

Social Security payments are paid out according to your birthday. If your birthday is on or before the 10th day of the month, you'll receive your payment on the second Wednesday. If you were born between the 11th and 20th day of the month, you will receive your payment on the third Wednesday. For birthdays between the 21st and the last day of the month, your payment will arrive on the fourth Wednesday. Example: Passing away on August 24th means no money will be deposited on the second, third or fourth Wednesday of the next month. If the payment has already been deposited, it will be removed electronically or must be repaid as soon as the SSA learns of the death.

Primary Worker and Early Benefits

Any person (Primary Worker) who has earned his or her 40 credits can currently receive Social Security income either early, beginning at age 62, or at *full retirement age*, which from the years 2005 through 2017 is 66 years old, and 67 from 2018 on. For each year between age 62 and age 70 that you delay your benefit, your monthly benefit will increase. You can delay taking Social Security up to any age, but when you reach 70, your benefit amount will cease growing. Individuals who choose to receive early retirement between ages 62 and 66 (age 67 starting 2018), will see a resulting benefit decrease of about 20-30% per month. (You get less because, presumably, you will receive your benefits longer and this stretches out those payments.)

Because Social Security was intended to save elderly non-workers from impoverishment, there are *penalties* if you take early benefits and also continue to work. In 2017, the Social Security Administration currently deducts $1 of benefits for every $2 earned above $16,920 per year if you are between the ages of 62 and your full retirement age of 66 or 67 (depending on your birth year). During the calendar year in which you reach your full retirement age, $1 in $3 is deducted, but the earnings limit is higher, at $44,880 per year (2017 amounts). From full retirement age onward, there is no deduction from your Social Security benefit due to income you receive from working. However, your Social Security benefit is *income* and part of it will be taxed.

Taxation of Social Security Income

Unlike regular income from working which is all taxable, a portion of your Social Security benefit *may* also be counted as taxable income for your federal income taxes. If Social Security is your only source of income, it will not be taxable.

If you are single and earn $25,000 to $34,000 a year, or are married and earn $32,000 to $44,000 a year from all sources, including investments, then *up to* 50% of your Social Security benefit will be taxed as income.

If you are single and you earn over $34,000 a year or are married and earn more than $44,000 a year, *up to* 85% of your Social Security benefit will be counted as taxable and will be added to the dollar amount of all of the rest of your taxable income.

No more than 85% of your benefit will be taxable regardless of income. Since you know that you will be taxed on part of your Social Security income, you may want to factor that in when deciding when to start taking Social Security income because that income could bump you up into a higher tax bracket.

A dwindling number of states tax some or all of a Social Security benefit at the state level. Check with your State Department of Taxation to determine whether your state taxes Social Security benefits.

Windfall Elimination Provision (WEP)

The Windfall Elimination Provision (WEP) affects how the amount of your retirement or disability benefit is calculated if you receive a pension from employment in which no Social Security payments were withheld. The maximum reduction under the WEP formula published for 2016 is about $428 per month. (The program is being considered for an overhaul as of 2017). This provision does not apply if you earned at least 30 credits from work in which Social Security was deducted, no matter how much you earned from other work. For example, employees who worked overseas for a foreign employer would not necessarily have had Social Security taken out of their pay. Federal employees hired before 1986 may have participated in the Civil Service Retirement System which could offset Social Security benefit amounts. State and local government employees may also be affected because local governments sometimes choose alternative pensions instead of having workers pay into the federal government's Social Security retirement plan. Certain railroad workers may also be affected because there was no system set up for them to pay into Social Security before 1973. If you think any of these issues may affect you, please call 1-800-772-1213 to see how your benefits may be offset.

Be aware that the federal government can withhold part of your Social Security and other federal or military benefits, or garnish wages if you owe federal debts and penalties, regardless of how old these debts are. This is done through the Treasury Offset Program (TOP). Debts older than 10 years were formerly unreachable. That is no longer the case. At last count, the first $750 of monthly federal benefits (such as social security income) is sheltered from this rule. After that, the lesser of either 15% of the whole benefit amount, or the whole amount by which the benefit exceeds about $750 can be withheld monthly.

Dependents Benefits

Potential dependent beneficiaries include:

- current spouses,

- divorced spouses who were married to you for at least 10 years and not remarried before age 60, unless that remarriage legally ended before age 60, and

- eligible children (unmarried minors up to age 18 or still attending high school, or disabled children provided that their disability was diagnosed before age 22).

Qualifying dependent beneficiaries can receive up to 50% of the Primary Worker's benefit amount or their own benefit amount if they are 62 or older, whichever is *greater*.

Example: A dependent spouse may receive approximately 35% of the Primary Worker's benefit amount at age 62 but will receive closer to 50% as he or she approaches age 66.

Another example: a man, age 69, collects $1000 in Social Security benefits per month. His wife, age 66, worked too, but her benefit amount based on her own work record would be $450 a month. She can collect 50% of her husband's benefit amount instead which would be $500.

Their disabled adult son, age 40, never worked so his own record would yield $0. He can collect 50% of his dad's benefit amount which would be $500 a month.

The man's ex-wife, age 67, can also collect 50% of his benefit amount if she has no work record which would provide her with a benefit above 50% of her ex-husband's benefit. She will receive whatever is the higher amount, even if she never worked outside the home. (More on ex-spouses below in the "Maximum Family Benefits" section.)

Survivors Benefits

Social Security Survivors benefits can be thought of as a life insurance policy for qualifying individuals who survive your death. A widow or widower at full retirement age may be able to receive 100% of a deceased spouse's benefit amount. Unlike regular Social Security retirement benefits, which require you to be 62 or older, a surviving spouse may receive benefits as early as age 60.

A spouse of a deceased primary worker between the ages of 60 and 66 would receive approximately 70% to 99% of the deceased spouse's benefit amount.

If the surviving spouse is *disabled*, benefits can begin as early as age 50.

Surviving spouses and ex-spouses *of any age* can receive benefits if they care for a legal child of the deceased spouse or ex-spouse, who is either younger than age 16 or disabled and entitled to benefits on the deceased spouse's record.

Unmarried children younger than 18 or still attending high school can receive 75% of a deceased parent's benefit amount. Disabled children can receive benefits at any age if they were disabled before age 22 and remain disabled.

Dependent parents of a deceased individual may receive benefits if they are age 62 or older. For parents to qualify as dependents, the deceased individual would have had to be providing at least one-half of his or her parent's support at the time of death. Proof of this support must be provided to the Social Security Administration within two years of the individual's death.

As with dependents benefits, a survivor will receive either the benefit which is based on his or her own record, or a percentage of the deceased's benefit, whichever is greater. The percentage varies with the survivor's age.

Maximum Family Benefits

With all the possible recipients of benefit amounts based on the work record of one Primary Worker, there is a limit to the total amount of benefits that can be paid out each month to qualifying recipients.

The limit varies according to what benefit percentages various family members receive, but it is generally between 150% and 180% of the Primary Worker's benefit amount. If the maximum is reached, the payments to each of the many recipients may be proportionally reduced. If this happens, a beneficiary might find that claiming on his or her own record, or that of another eligible family member's record, yields a higher amount.

An exception to the above rule is <u>that payments to a divorced spouse</u> are exempt from this 150% to 180% rule which would potentially reduce the rest of the family's benefit amount, (unless the divorced spouse is taking benefits and also caring for the child of the deceased individual and that child is receiving benefits). Therefore, the share of any ex-spouse's benefits will not tip the scale over the Maximum Family Benefit amounts and cause other family members to have reduced payments.

Because age 70 is the latest retirement age, and because no state recognizes marriage before teenage years, there can be no more than five successive spousal benefits in ten-year intervals. (That means a person can have no more than five ex-spouses receiving benefits on his or her record.)

Social Security Disability Insurance (SSDI)

The Social Security Administration has two programs that provide benefits based on *disability or blindness*. One is the Social Security Disability Insurance program (SSDI), and the second is the Supplemental Security Income program (SSI). Disabled people often refer to "my social security payment" without distinguishing between SSDI and SSI. In terms of both health care benefits and asset requirements, however, the differences are *very important*.

Social Security Disability Insurance (SSDI) is available to people who qualify on their own record or someone else's record for Social Security and who are disabled and are earning less than $1,170 per month for 2017. The $1,170 refers only to income from employment. Beneficiaries can have investment earnings without being disqualified. The benefit amount varies in accordance with the number of work credits the individual has.

There is a trial work period for disabled beneficiaries who are working and making more than $840 a month. The trial period lasts for nine months, which do not have to be consecutive, within a maximum 60-month window, during which time full benefits will be received regardless of how much the disabled person earns. After that trial work period, benefits may be received as long as the disabled individual does not earn more than $1,170 a month. The disability must be expected to last at least one year or result in early death.

In order to qualify as "disabled," an individual will generally have to prove his or her disability through a process with the SSA staff. However, some disabilities are so grave that they automatically qualify an individual as being "disabled." These disabilities can be found on the *List of Compassionate Allowances Conditions*, available on the Social Security Administration website, <u>www.ssa.gov</u>.

The rule for *blind* individuals is different. They may receive SSDI as long as they do not earn more than $1,950 a month for 2017.

There is no *asset* test for SSDI. One can be a millionaire and still qualify. The same is not true of SSI (see below).

For individuals who are disabled or blind and receiving SSDI, their disability benefit amount will convert to the higher of their regular Social Security benefit amount or their SSDI amount when they reach full retirement age.

For many disabled persons, obtaining even a small amount of SSDI is extremely important because it also qualifies them for Medicare. As a practical matter, *Medicare* benefits are generally superior to those provided to SSI recipients under *Medicaid*. Some individuals qualify for income under both SSDI and SSI, and also qualify for health benefits under both Medicare and Medicaid.

SSA staff will determine if an individual has been working "recently enough" and "long enough" to qualify for SSDI. Therefore, individuals cannot necessarily decide years after the onset of a disability to apply for benefits, or they may not be found eligible.

The *50% to 85% tax rule*, the *maximum monthly family benefit rule*, the *Windfall Elimination Provision, Worker's Compensation* payments, and *certain pensions* can also change an SSDI benefit amount.

Supplemental Security Income (SSI)

Supplemental Security Income (SSI) is a cash assistance program available to those who are aged, blind or disabled, including children, and who have very limited income and resources. Generally, an individual must have no more than $2,000 in resources and a couple must have no more than $3,000.

The federal government funds SSI from general tax revenues, not from withheld Social Security taxes. SSI is a welfare program providing income, not an insurance program like SSDI, to which an individual contributed through payroll taxes. However, SSI is administered by the Social Security Administration. The method by which a person is found to be disabled is governed by the same Social Security Administration criteria for both SSDI and SSI.

The maximum payment for SSI in 2017 is $735 per month per individual and $1,103 for an eligible individual with an eligible spouse, AKA "eligible couple". It is possible to receive regular Social Security benefits or Social Security Disability Insurance (SSDI) while also receiving Supplemental Security Income (SSI) without a reduction in either amount if the grand total is still under the SSI threshold. Otherwise, SSDI payments reduce SSI income dollar for dollar except for the first $20 of unearned income.

If you are eligible for SSI and are under age 65, you are also eligible for Medicaid health coverage. When you reach age 65, or younger if you are receiving SSDI, you can also qualify for Medicare. In that case, Medicaid can pay your Medicare Parts B and D premiums, deductibles and co-pays.

If someone receiving Social Security payments cannot manage his or her funds, such as someone who has Alzheimer's Disease, a family member or friend may apply to be a "representative payee." A representative payee will be allowed to receive and spend payments on behalf of the recipient. SSA will require you to account to the SSA for every penny to assure that the benefit is spent or saved for future use for the legal recipient.

Death Benefits

There is a one-time death benefit of $255 originally intended to pay for funeral services. It won't cover that now! Congress doesn't seem to have found the heart to get rid of the benefit, so had settled for simply not raising it. Applications for this benefit must be made within two years of the date of death. It is generally paid to the widow or widower of the deceased or a qualifying dependent child or dependent parent of the deceased.

OTHER FUNDING FOR OLD AGE: WHEN SOCIAL SECURITY ISN'T ENOUGH

Retirement Funding Overview

It is widely suggested that you will need to plan to have 60%-85% of your pre-retirement income for approximately 30 years after you retire, although everyone's situation is different. A "to do" list includes the following:

- Overestimate your life expectancy;
- Underestimate your level of health;
- Overestimate inflation; and
- Underestimate the rate of investment returns.

In addition to Social Security and Veterans Benefits discussed below, you should discuss with your financial advisor whether and to what extent you should participate in Individual Retirement Accounts (IRAs), Qualified Retirement Plans such as 401(k)s, use regular savings and investment accounts, whether you should use a reverse mortgage, buy an annuity, buy long-term care insurance, etc.

Your tax advisor can also be very helpful. Be sure to ask for a face-to-face meeting to discuss your finances and your retirement goals. Tax advisors can assist you in deciding when to start taking retirement plan distributions and can help you avoid penalties on such distributions.

Your tax advisor can also help you with deductions. For example, most money paid out for medical expenses, LTC insurance premiums, medical transportation, medical equipment, home improvements for medical reasons (to name a few) can be deductible if you itemize your taxes. Historically individuals have been able to claim deductions for out of pocket medical expenses that exceed 7.5% of gross income. As of January 1, 2017, that number changed to 10% of gross income. Keep records of your charitable contributions; they are tax deductible. If you provide care for your parents or other disabled adult, you might be able to claim that person as a dependent for income tax purposes.

Retirement planning in general is a vastly expansive and complicated field. It is strongly recommended that you consult with your own financial advisor regarding the many retirement planning opportunities that exist. Anything more than the sampling set forth below is beyond the scope of this book. Speak to an advisor such as a Certified Public

Accountant (CPA), Certified Financial Planner (CFP), Certified Private Wealth Advisor (CPWA) or similarly qualified professional about your options.

Regular Individual Retirement Accounts (IRAs)

An IRA is an investment account that you can contribute to on a regular basis. Subject to limits you should discuss with your financial advisor, your IRA contributions are tax deductible. Funds in the IRA build up and earn income over time. The major advantage of an IRA over a regular investment account is that income earned on assets held in the IRA are not subject to income taxes at the time the income is earned, thus allowing the IRA account to increase in value free of current income taxes.

However, to benefit from the IRA you must be prepared to leave the money in the IRA account until you are at least age 59 ½. If you withdraw assets from your IRA prior to turning age 59 ½, the withdrawal will be subject to a 10% penalty in addition to income taxes. There are a few exceptions to this penalty rule such as withdrawals for payment of health insurance premiums while unemployed or for purchasing a first home. However, if you do make a withdrawal, even if it is not subject to a penalty, it is still subject to income taxes.

You can continue to contribute tax-deductible payments to your IRA until you are age 70 ½. However, by April 1 of the year after you turn 70 ½ you must begin to make regular withdrawals from your IRA even if you would prefer to leave all the funds in the IRA to continue growing tax free.

The money you paid into the IRA was tax deductible; the withdrawals will be subject to ordinary income tax. The withdrawals you are required to make beginning after you turn 70 ½ are known as "required minimum distributions" (RMDs). RMD amounts are computed based on life expectancy tables. After age 70 ½ you can withdraw more than the minimum, up to the whole balance in the account, without penalty. But everything you withdraw will be treated as *ordinary income* for tax purposes.

The maximum that you can contribute to an IRA changes from year to year and is different for investors of different ages. You can also create an IRA for your non-working spouse. Check with your financial and tax advisors for details.

If an IRA owner dies with assets remaining in his IRA account, the funds can either be paid out in a lump sum to the person he designates as the IRA beneficiary, or the beneficiary can "stretch out" payments, thereby continuing to benefit from the tax deferred earnings on IRA assets. These issues must be discussed with your financial and tax advisors.

Roth IRA

A Roth IRA is similar to a regular IRA except that income tax payment issues are reversed. With the regular IRA, you took a tax deduction when you put money in but were taxed when you made withdrawals. A Roth Ira is the other way around. Your contributions are not tax deductible, but when you make withdrawals, the income will be tax-free provided that the owner is at least 59 ½ and the account has been open five years from the first day of the year that the Roth IRA was set up. As with a regular IRA, there are penalties for withdrawals taken before age 59 ½ with exceptions that apply to all IRAs.

Unlike the policy governing regular IRAs, you can continue to contribute to a Roth IRA after age 70 ½. With a Roth IRA, moreover, you are not required to make withdrawals on any particular schedule. The maximum annual amount you can contribute to all of your IRSs combined, traditional and Roth, is $5,500-$6,500, depending on your age.

401(k) (aka 401K)

401(k) plans are retirement plans similar to IRAs, but they are set up through your employer. Up to certain limits, both the employee and the employer can contribute. The same "age" rules and penalties apply as for IRAs. However, the maximum annual contributions by employees and employers are different.

Life Insurance

A life insurance policy pays a pre-determined sum of money to the person or persons you designate as beneficiaries. Life insurance can be used as a way to reward a family caregiver who has taken care of you during a long or terminal illness. It can also be made payable to a special needs trust for a disabled child. That disabled child will need more resources for his special needs after his parent(s) has died.

Premiums for term life insurance are paid monthly or annually for a designated time period, i.e., the term. You can stop paying at any time but there will be no refunds of what you've already paid. When the term expires, the premiums due for the next term might increase substantially because during the next term, you will be older. Term life policies do not build up any cash value. If you stop making premium payments on a term life policy, your beneficiary will receive no life insurance payout. You will receive no credit for payments you have already made. It is this reality, however, that makes premium payments for "term coverage" less expensive than those for whole life policies.

"Permanent" or "whole life" insurance policies, continue in effect as long as the premiums are paid. Premiums build up a cash value within this type of policy. If you pay for a long enough time, the cash value of the policy can become large enough that the policy is considered "paid up" and you do not have to make any additional premium payments. You can also borrow against the built-up cash value of a whole life policy without jeopardizing the insurance. If you die while you have an outstanding loan, the insurance company will simply deduct the amount of the loan balance from the death benefit to be received by your beneficiaries.

During the AIDS epidemic in the 1980s, some AIDS victims who were in a terminal condition found a creative way to fund their care in their last days. They would sell their life insurance policies, whose premiums they could no longer afford anyway, in what is called a Life Settlement or "Viatical Settlement." The purchaser would pay the insured, dying seller an amount which could be fairly large but would always be significantly less than the amount of the death benefit. The new owner of the policy would then designate himself as the death benefit beneficiary, continue to pay the premiums until the death of the seller, and collect the death benefit when the seller died. The term "viatical" is derived from the Latin word for life. It describes the sale of the policy during the lifetime of the insured. Thus, these options can turn life insurance into cash for a terminally or chronically ill person. The purchase price paid to the insured can be used for any purpose, but the prior-named beneficiaries then have no right to the money after the insured's death.

Caution: Some types of viatical life insurance sales have come under government scrutiny for abuses wherein "investors" persuade an elderly person to take out a new life insurance policy with a very large death benefit funded by a large lump sum premium paid by the investors. The elderly person receives a lump sum which is a small fraction of the value of the policy's death benefit. Then the investors sit back and wait for the elderly person to die. Some courts have invalidated such arrangements because the purchaser/beneficiaries of the policy had no "insurable interest" in the elderly person. Insurable interests are held by persons who hope the insured will **not** die, such as family members and business partners

Annuities

Annuities are contracts between an insurance company and a purchaser wherein the purchaser gives the insurance company a lump sum of money in exchange for the insurance company's promise to pay the purchaser a certain amount of money in monthly installments.

An "immediate annuity" starts paying out immediately but in lower monthly payments because the insurance company has less time to invest the lump sum. Monthly annuity payments which do not begin to pay out until sometime in the future, i.e., "deferred annuities," will result in higher monthly payments to the purchaser.

Payments to purchase an annuity can be made in a lump sum or in periodic payments and can grow at fixed or variable rates. "Fixed annuities" pay out the same amount each month; "variable annuities" will pay variable payments based on applicable interest rates and formulas.

An advantage of annuities is that they can guarantee income for life. Thus, if you live long enough you might receive more in payments than actually went into your annuity account. If you die prematurely, the annuity company will provide a death benefit to whomever you designate.

The biggest downside to a fixed annuity is that fixed monthly payments do not keep up with inflation. Other disadvantages of annuities generally include high fees and loss of liquidity. There are many variations of annuities with different risks and benefits. Talk this over with your financial advisor to determine whether an annuity is a good choice for you. Be sure to consider the variations before deciding to purchase an annuity.

Home Equity

For those with substantial equity in their homes, looking into refinancing at a lower rate or obtaining a home equity line of credit may be a good option.

Reverse Mortgages

Many people want to age in place but have limited income to pay expenses, even though they may own their homes free and clear of any mortgage, or fairly close to that. Their homes might be worth hundreds of thousands of dollars, but that equity is not liquid and can't help them pay for a home health aide. They are "house poor." The answer for some of those people is a Home Equity Conversion Mortgage (HECM), usually called a reverse mortgage.

A reverse mortgage is a financial planning tool by which a financial institution makes payments to you instead of the other way around. The money paid to you, either in monthly installments, a lump sum, or as a line of credit you can write checks on, is a loan to you secured by the equity in your home. When you die, or move out for any reason, the amount you owe must be paid back. This is usually done by selling the house. Upon the sale of the house, you or your heirs can keep any money left over after paying off the reverse mortgage balance. If heirs want to keep the house, they can essentially "buy" it by paying off the amount of the loan. With a reverse mortgage, your home remains your home for you to live in for the rest of your life if you so choose and there is no restriction on how you use the funds.

In 2017, the current maximum reverse mortgage amount you can receive is $636,150. That high amount is typically granted in what the FHA considers to be "high cost" areas, such as a few large US cities. The current borrowing limit for an area deemed to be "low cost" is $275,665.
You can search for a list of these areas on www.hud.gov.

Reverse mortgages are available to those over the age of 62 with substantial equity in their homes in addition to some other rules that underwent considerable changes in 2015 (see www.hud.gov and search for HECM).

You may have seen TV commercials that say that you can qualify for a reverse mortgage "regardless of your credit history". That has been true, but is not any longer.

Unlike in the past, applicants have to meet credit and income requirements, things like credit score, and whether someone has borrowed on a home line of credit 12 months prior to applying, may affect qualification. The reason is that lenders have experienced losses on their investments. A common issue is that the borrower fails to pay property taxes generating a lien on the property. Another, is the borrower fails to pay homeowner's insurance and if the property is damaged or destroyed, there is no way for the mortgage lender to recoup the loss.

The deal you get (how much and at what interest rate) will depend on three main things:

- the age of the borrower,
- prevailing interest rates, and
- the condition and value of the residence.

Mortgage companies use projected life expectancies in determining amounts of payments; therefore, the older the borrower, the higher the likelihood he or she will receive larger payments. Reverse mortgage loans offered by Federal Housing Administration (FHA) approved lenders are insured by the FHA. To assure that you are properly informed about the details of the reverse mortgage, the government now requires that you participate in a reverse mortgage training session and receive a "certificate of counseling" before you apply.

If you do not meet the income or credit requirements, there is an alternative way to obtain a reverse mortgage. In order for lenders to ensure that borrowers without solid financial standing will keep up with property taxes and homeowners insurance, a new "set-aside" option will be available. Funds for taxes and insurance are taken out of the reverse mortgage loan amount (whatever amount you qualified for) and put into a "Fully-Funded Life Expectancy Set-Aside." The amount set aside is determined by a formula to calculate how much would be needed for the remaining lifetime of a borrower.

A big draw for people interested in a reverse mortgage is that the monthly payments to you *can* exceed the value of the home if you live in the home long enough. You never have to move; but if you do move, or sell your home, you must repay what you have borrowed. You are guaranteed payments for life or until you move out.

If the sale of the house, after you die or move, does not produce a sufficient amount to repay what you borrowed, the reverse mortgage company takes the loss. When you die, the repayment of the reverse mortgage is a debt of your estate. Your heirs will have the first right of refusal to repay the loan and purchase the house as their own if they so choose. Otherwise, your estate sells the home to repay the reverse mortgage and your heirs will receive the amount, if any, left over after the reverse mortgage loan is paid back. If the home sells for less than what you owe the reverse mortgage company, the difference is the reverse mortgage lender's loss. It is a significant benefit that if the home sells for more than the mortgage repayment balance, your heirs get to keep the excess amount.

The reverse mortgage funding option can be very helpful for individuals who wish to continue living in their own homes and need liquid funds for day-to-day expenses and for caregiving services. Because of the rates and high fees, it is advisable to consider a reverse mortgage only if other sources of funding long-term care have been depleted and you do not want to sell the home in order to pay for an assisted living facility or nursing home. At this time the IRS does not consider the proceeds from reverse mortgages to be taxable income. However, because every situation is different, you should consult with your tax advisor.

Reverse mortgages often have very high up-front fees. Those may be a price some are willing to pay to stay in their own homes.

Important Note: If you want your Trustee or POA to have the power to obtain a reverse mortgage for you, ensure that your estate planning or elderlaw attorney inserts specific language into your documents in the section that deals with Real Property.

VETERANS BENEFITS

There are four United States Department of Veterans Affairs (VA) plans that veterans should be aware of:

- Veterans Pension,
- Veterans Disability Compensation,
- Aid and Attendance,
- Housebound Pension.

It has been estimated that approximately 12.4 million seniors, approximately a third of the US over-65 population, could possibly qualify for some VA benefits. That is the number of war veterans and/or their living or surviving spouses who might meet eligibility requirements, although far fewer are currently taking advantage of these programs.

The Department of Veterans Affairs website also lists:
Other Benefits: VA provides additional housing and insurance benefits to Veterans with disabilities, including Adapted Housing grants, Service-Disable Veterans' Insurance, and Veterans' Mortgage Life Insurance. See www.va.gov for more information.

Income for VA Purposes (IVAP)

IVAP is "Income for VA Purposes" as calculated by the Department of Veterans Affairs. In order to understand the possible benefit packages, one must first understand how the VA determines a veteran's income for the purpose of calculating possible eligibility.

The IVAP calculation takes a veteran's total income (including, but not limited to, Social Security, pensions, IRAs, rental income, interest, dividends, etc.), subtracts his or her out-of-pocket medical expenses and comes up with the IVAP amount. For example, if a veteran has monthly income of $1600 and out-of-pocket medical expenses of $3,000, the IVAP dollar amount will be $0; as long as the difference between total income and out-of-pocket medical expenses comes out to $0 or less the IVAP number will be zero. As long as a veteran's IVAP is $0, he or she will receive the maximum dollar amount set forth below depending on marital status and dependents.

The VA calculates items under "medical expenses" that are traditionally not considered "medical" for the purposes of Medicare and other health insurance. These include medical insurance premiums, unreimbursed prescription expenses, dental, medical supplies, procedures under medical advice, nursing home fees, home health fees, assisted living fees, etc. Any portion of these types of costs that a veteran paid for out-of-pocket after any coverage was applied by other benefit plans counts as "medical expenses" for the IVAP calculation. If the IVAP is over $0 but under the maximum possible benefit amount, the veteran will receive the difference.

Example: If monthly income is $1600 and medical expenses are $1200, the IVAP is $400. These calculations are for informational purposes; the actual dollar amounts may be subject to changes based on more in-depth rules. For instance, "medical expenses" must exceed 5% of the Maximum Annual Pension Rate (MAPR).

In addition to income, some assets will be factored in when determining benefit eligibility. As is also true of Medicaid, the family home and car are not counted as family assets. Life insurance and personal property, among others, are also uncountable.

The VA will not publish a dollar amount of assets which would be "too high" for a veteran to qualify. They will likely look at the age of the veteran and how long his or her assets may last as part of their determination.

VA benefit plans may change and may contain some complex rules. Below are current general guidelines as of 2017. Contact the Department of Veterans Affairs, the American Legion, veteran's associations, or an elder law attorney for more information.

Veterans Pension

Many veterans of wartime service are unaware that if they are age 65 or older, and on a limited income, they may qualify for a Veterans Pension *without* being disabled.

To qualify for the Veterans Pension, the veteran must have been discharged from service under other than dishonorable conditions after having served 90 days or more of active duty with at least one day of service during a period of wartime. However, if a veteran enlisted after September 7, 1980, the required service time jumps to 24 months, with one day during a wartime period, in most cases.

A Veterans Pension is a benefit that pays you the difference between your countable family income and a set yearly income limit. A common example used is of Joe, a single veteran, whose annual income is $5000. The 2017 annual income minimum for a single veteran is $12,907. To determine Joe's pension, subtract his annual income of $5,000 from his $12,907 income limit, which equals an *annual* pension rate of $7,907. Joe will receive a *monthly* pension check of approximately $659. The income limit for married couples is $16,902.

The resulting approximate base annual pension amounts for 2017 are as follows:

- $12,907 for a single veteran
- $16,902 for a married veteran or a veteran with one dependent
- $8,656 for a surviving spouse of a veteran
- $11,330 for a surviving spouse with one dependent

Veterans Disability Compensation

If you are a wartime veteran with a limited income and are no longer able to work, you may qualify for a Veterans Disability Pension *at any age.* To qualify for Veterans Disability Compensation, a veteran must be 65 or older, *or if younger*, permanently and totally disabled, with countable family income below a yearly limit set by law.

There are gifting prohibitions that closely match Medicaid rules to prevent people from giving money away to family members or others. The VA will work with SSA to verify continued eligibility, in case any benefit adjustments need to be made.

For disabled veterans 65 and over, a compensation amount is calculated using a somewhat complex formula. However, the basis of that formula is called a "Disability Range" that begins with a VA assigning you a disability rating in the form of a percentage. Example: A 30% disability rating from a particular condition would be multiplied by another percentage signifying your overall health, such as 100% per those in good health. The resulting number will generate a dollar amount. This dollar amount will vary in terms of numbers of dependents (which can change due to divorces, births etc.). The disability rating is also not permanent because the extent to which a disability effects your functioning can change over time.

The Veterans Disability Compensation benefit provides a benefit amount ranging from about $133 to $3,330 monthly for a single veteran with a particular disability rating, and possibly more depending on marital and dependent status. Veterans must have had injuries or diseases that originated while on active duty or were made worse by active military service. Additionally, certain veterans whose disability resulted from VA health care problems may also receive this compensation. Some disabled veterans may even qualify for additional amounts for severe disabilities such as loss of limb or having a severely disabled spouse. These benefits are tax free.

Veterans Aid and Attendance (A&A)

Veterans Aid and Attendance (A&A) is a program that provides a tax-free lifelong benefit via direct deposit to a qualifying claimant and/or his or her spouse over age 65 (and occasionally dependent children). To qualify, a veteran must already be eligible under the Veterans Pension qualifications listed above. In addition, a veteran must have certain physical health limitations and meet a low-income threshold. Physically, a qualified veteran must:

- require the aid of another person in order to perform personal functions required in everyday living (ADLs);

- OR the veteran is bedridden in that his or her disability or disabilities require that he or she remain in bed apart from any prescribed course of convalescence or treatment;

- OR the veteran is a patient in a nursing home due to physical or mental incapacity;

- OR the veteran is blind or so nearly-blind as to have corrected visual acuity of 5/200 or less in both eyes or concentric contraction of the visual field to five degrees or less.

The income minimums for the A&A benefits for a single veteran with no dependents is *about* $21,531 per year; thus, the veteran will receive Aid and Attendance benefits equal to the difference between his or her actual annual income and the $21,531 per year. The countable family income limit for a veteran with one dependent, or who is married, is approximately $25,525 per year.

The resulting approximate base A&A annual benefit amounts for 2017 are:

- $21,531 for unmarried veterans,
- $25,525 for veterans who are married or a vet with one dependent,
- $13,836 for a surviving spouse of a veteran,
- $34,153 for two veterans married to each other both needing A&A.

Note: these dollar amounts apply when it is the veteran who needs assistance. There is a benefit, not technically under the A&A benefit, that allows a veteran to file as a "veteran with a sick spouse" and be eligible to receive up to about $1,330 a month.

Housebound Benefit (HB)

A veteran's Housebound Benefit (HB) is also paid *in addition to* the regular monthly veterans pension. Like the A&A benefits, Housebound Benefits may not be paid without eligibility for the original Veterans Pension.

A veteran may be eligible for Housebound Benefits when the veteran has:

- a single permanent disability evaluated as 100% disabling
- AND due to such disability, he or she is permanently and substantially confined to his or her immediate premises,
- OR the veteran has a single permanent disability evaluated as 100% disabling
- AND another disability or disabilities evaluated as 60% or more disabling.

A veteran cannot receive both Aid and Attendance and Housebound Benefits at the same time.

The approximate annual maximum HB annual benefits for 2017 are:

- $15,733 for an unmarried veteran,
- $19,770 for a veteran who is married or has one dependent,
- $22,634 for two veterans married to each other who both need HB
- $10,580 for a surviving spouse of a veteran

Applications for A&A or HB require detailed and verifiable information; they must be done correctly to ensure no delay in enrollment. Just as elder law attorneys are essential for help with Medicaid applications, there are many attorneys, organizations and associations which can assist in maximizing a veteran's chances of having his or her application approved. Many provide this service free of charge. To an increasing extent, elder law attorneys are also developing expertise in the area of Veterans Benefits. Contact the U.S. Department of Veterans Affairs, the American Legion, or a veteran's association for more information. Additionally, some private financial planning groups offer services to help veterans apply for these benefits for free, although they may also be interested in offering advice about what to do with any other assets you may have.

NORMAL COGNITIVE DECLINE

There are a few cognitive changes that do appear to occur across the board when we age which are not tied to a disease process. Healthy seniors may experience decline in four areas: 1) speed of mental processing; 2) retention of new information; 3) reaction time; and, 4) vision and hearing (which can be mistaken for cognitive defects).

Speed of Mental Processing: Seniors score lower than younger people on tests of general mental ability. However, this is not due to a decline in mental ability. Seniors take in and process information more slowly, and therefore they take longer to complete the exams. When given more time, seniors process information just as well as younger people.

Retention of New Information: Because of the "speed" issue, seniors may be less able to store new material that is presented rapidly. Seniors also may take longer to recall information. When speed is removed from the learning equation, the discrepancy between older and younger adults disappears.

Reaction Time: Seniors' reflexes do slow down with normal aging. This may affect not only performance of cognitive activities but also physical activities that require rapid shifts in attention (like driving a car).

Vision and Hearing: A senior who cannot hear or see well cannot store or recall information as well and this may be mistaken for cognitive disability. Using hearing aids, glasses and other assistive devices can maximize the comprehension and retention of information.

Vision loss can result from alterations that occur to the structure of the eye over time including the lens being yellowed, opaque, and less flexible as well as pupils shrinking and responding less to light. People with reduced visual acuity are much more likely to fall or to have multiple falls than are people with normal vision. The odds of hip fracture are also far greater for people with reduced visual acuity.

There is a free resource for Vision impairment through your state's Department of the Blind and Vision Impaired. With a diagnosis of vision impairment, this Department can have an Occupational Therapist come out to the home and do an assessment of the individuals daily functioning with their visual impairment. They will then recommend assistive devices and modifications of the home to ensure safety and ease of daily functioning, which will increase independence. A lot of these items would be covered under Medicare or supplemental insurance. They can also assist with setting up Talking Books, which is a free library service for books on tape. The Talking Books device is easy for older adults to use and can be a pleasant replacement when they are no longer able to read.

Hearing is affected by normal aging over time due to changes such as the death of hair cells in the inner ear. Men and people exposed to long-term noise are affected the most.

> Comic Relief: Three retirees, each with hearing loss, were playing golf one day. One remarked, "Windy, isn't it?" "No," the second man replied, "It's Thursday." The third man chimed in, "So am I! Let's have a beer!"

Although that joke may be amusing, it highlights an important issue, which is that hearing loss can cause seniors to appear confused, when in reality they just did not hear something correctly.

To recap, it is important to be aware of these four areas of normal aging because they can have real effects on cognitive function. However, also remember that most seniors' intellects function well, though their approach to learning and recall may need to be altered to fully express that intellect.

COGNITIVE DEFECTS AND DISEASES

A range of cognitive defects and diseases exists that may affect us as we age that are NOT considered part of the *normal* aging process. These are addressed below.

Delirium

Delirium is confusion that begins suddenly and may vary from slight to severe within hours. Individuals with delirium cannot pay attention or think clearly. Delirium is usually temporary and reversible. Some causes are: changes in medications, stroke, dehydration, stress and infections such as a urinary tract infection (UTI), which can be very serious if not treated. When symptoms of confusion arise or progress rapidly, check with a doctor immediately. Even if an individual has dementia, *do not assume* rapid changes in symptoms are normal.

Mild Cognitive Impairment (MCI)

Mild cognitive impairment (MCI) is a state of progressive memory loss after the age of 50 that does not rise to the diagnostic level of dementia. MCI produces memory deficits that are abnormal for the age and education level of the sufferer. However, these individuals can still manage without assistance. Statistics for how many people suffer from MCI are difficult to pin down and thus far MCI has generally been studied only in smaller groups. An unknown percentage of MCI is an earlier or pre-state of Alzheimer's Disease.

Dementia

Dementia is NOT a part of normal aging. It is a set of symptoms indicating a possible cause, such as Alzheimer's Disease, Vascular Dementia, Lewy Body etc. A useful analogy can be found in the textbook of the Society for Certified Senior Advisors (CSA). It is the "cold symptom" analogy. Three people have cold symptoms: one caused by a virus, another by bacteria, and the third, allergies. These are different causes of similar symptoms. Some treatments, such as decongestants, will be similar for all three, and some will be different, such as the use of antibiotics for a bacterial infection. Determining the cause of the dementia is important; it might be due to a reversible condition. Dementia is the primary reason seniors are admitted to nursing homes.

The diagnosis of dementia is given when these criteria are met:

- deficits in memory that are short term (a few minutes to a few hours, such as what one had for breakfast) AND long term (weeks to months such as who is President and the names of grandchildren);

- deficits in ONE of the following areas:

- *Aphasia* - the inability to understand and use language, such as identifying common objects;

- *Agnosia* - the inability to visually recognize familiar objects or people;

- *Apraxia* - difficulty with physical activity that is not caused by a physical ailment but rather by how the brain commences the movement, and

- *Difficulty with Executive Functioning* - problem-solving/abstract thinking, such as balancing a checkbook, the ability to understand irony, sarcasm and symbolism.

IF the above deficits interfere significantly with daily activities OR represent a significant deterioration from one's prior level of functioning AND no other medical condition can account for the symptoms THEN the diagnosis of dementia can be given. If your loved ones exhibit these symptoms, it is important to seek a medical diagnosis. Some dementia is treatable and some is irreversible.

Treatable or Temporary Dementia

Treatable dementia can appear in several forms: Toxic - due to alcohol, drug or heavy metal exposure; Metabolic - possibly from thyroid disease or vitamin B12 deficiency; Depression-Related-Pseudo-Dementia - because some depressive episodes can present with symptoms of dementia; and lastly, Medication-Induced - due to drug reactions, which is the most common cause of treatable dementia. (However, long-term drug or alcohol use can cause permanent brain damage that presents like dementia, ex: alcoholic dementia that is not reversible.)

As we all know, sleep is one of the most important things our body needs. Without sufficient sleep, our brain does not function properly. It can contribute to cognitive impairment, inability to pay attention, and even impaired decision making. (http://www.brainfacts.org/about-neuroscience/ask-an-expert/articles/2015/what-happens-to-your-brain-when-you-are-sleep-deprived/) Studies are now showing that regular sleep deprivation can contribute to the risk of developing cognitive impairment. Sleep disturbance is also a symptom of most dementias. Sometimes the sleep is disrupted regularly throughout the night, but other times individuals may not be able to get to sleep or stay asleep for very long and only get a few hours of sleep. There are other occurrences where the sleep cycle is reversed, so the individual sleeps during the day instead of at night. This can also contribute to sleep deprivation, because during the day they likely won't be able to get the amount of sleep they need as they will be going to appointments, eat, visit with people, etc. If someone who already has dementia is not getting the sleep they need, it can rapidly progress the symptoms associated with the cognitive impairment.

Irreversible Dementia

The causes of irreversible dementia include: Alzheimer's Disease (AD, the most common cause of dementia), Parkinson's Disease with Dementia (PDD), and Dementia with Lewy Bodies (DLB). Some patients with AD and PDD have been found to have clumps of protein in brain neurons. Vascular Dementia is caused by small strokes that decrease blood flow to the brain. Other causes of irreversible dementia can include infections, such as AIDS, or physical damage, such as head injury or brain tumor.

Frontotemporal Dementia

Frontotemporal Dementia (FTD) refers to a group of disorders that primarily affect the brain's frontal lobes (the areas behind the forehead) or its temporal lobes (the regions behind the ears). FTD was originally called Pick's Disease as it was named after Dr. Arnold Pick who first described in 1892 a patient with distinct symptoms affecting language. Some doctors do still refer to it as Pick's Disease. Frontotemporal disorders, frontotemporal degenerations and frontal lobe disorders are other terms used to describe FTD. The nerve cell damage caused by FTD leads to a loss of brain function in these areas. The result of this damage is a deterioration in behavior and personality, language difficulties, or changes in muscle or motor functions. No one test can identify FTD. It can be especially difficult to diagnose in its early stages as some of its symptoms overlap with other conditions. It is often misdiagnosed as a psychiatric problem or Alzheimer's Disease. The core of the diagnosis is the patient's symptoms and neurological exams. Age at diagnosis is a helpful clue as most people with FTD are diagnosed in their early 40s through early 60s. It is far less common in individuals over the age of 65, unlike for example Alzheimer's Disease, which is more common with advanced age. It is estimated that there may be 50,000 to 60,000 people in the United States with FTD, the majority of whom are between 45 and 65 years of age. There is no cure for FTD nor an effective way to slow its symptoms. Treatment consists of trying to manage the symptoms with medications and/or therapy. FTD is inherited in approximately thirty percent of all cases. Genetic counseling and testing is now available for individuals with this family history. The theory that traumatic brain injury such as from accidents or sport's injuries is currently an important focus of study.

Alzheimer's Disease (AD)

The Alzheimer's Association has published a list of ten warning signs for Alzheimer's Disease. If a person exhibits several of these symptoms, he or she should be evaluated by a physician:

- memory loss,
- challenges in planning or problem solving,
- difficulty completing familiar tasks,
- confusion with time and space (getting lost),
- trouble with visual images and spatial relationships,
- new problems with words, spoken and written,
- misplacing things and losing the ability to retrace steps,
- decreased or poor judgment,
- withdrawal from work or social activities, and
- changes in mood and personality.

Well over five million Americans have Alzheimer's Disease. That is almost equal to the entire population of Colorado.

Unless sufferers of AD die of some other illness before they reach Late-Stage AD, they will eventually die because they cease to eat, lose their ability to swallow and eventually slip into a coma or die of pneumonia or cardiac arrest. There are interim treatments for AD such as medications used to treat the cognitive effects of AD by working on the way the brain's nerve cells carry messages. Psychiatric medications can help with the behavioral and psychiatric symptoms of AD, such as hallucinations, outbursts, and emotional distress. Psychotherapy and behavioral intervention can be effective in helping patients process and cope with the emotional issues of the disease, thereby cutting down on depression, which can worsen symptoms.

It can be hard for AD sufferers to accept their diagnosis. As their illness progresses, they sometimes move from "covering" or making excuses for symptoms, such as not remembering things or people, to blaming others for misplacing things. They can become paranoid and belligerent. This illness can be very difficult for families to accept as well.

Caregivers of people with dementia have been found to suffer suppressed immune systems, increased rates of infectious illness, and a higher prevalence of major depression than non-caregivers. Seeking self-care such as support groups and counseling can alleviate common feelings of resentment, burden and lack of control.

See the Alzheimer's Association website, www.alz.org or, the Alzheimer's Foundation of America website www.alzfdn.org for more information.

In addition, The Alzheimer's Disease Education and Referral Center (ADEAR) is a free service under the National Institutes on Aging. You can reach a specialist to answer your specific questions, provide free publications, and give you referrals and resources Mondays through Fridays at 1-800-438-4380 or by email at adear@nia.nih.gov.

General tips for caring for people with dementia include:

- Be aware of overstimulation because people with AD are limited in processing incoming information and can become overwhelmed;

- Be aware of the risk factors of wandering, a dangerous issue for many with AD; use door alarms and other monitoring devices instead of locks which can be hazardous in a fire;

- When communicating with persons with AD or any dementia, understand that sufferers may say and do inappropriate things, may try to use non-verbal communication, or not be able to communicate at all. Look out for physical signs for what they need, such as whether or not they may be cold;

- Approach them from the front, speak slowly and keep eye contact.

When assisting or dealing with individuals with dementia, the **"Validation Therapy and Redirection Method"** can be helpful. Human instinct prompts us to correct people who are misstating facts or are unaware of the reality around them. Instead of correcting them, make a general statement validating how they feel about what they said, and then redirect them onto another topic.

Trying to correct the reality of an individual with dementia is not only fruitless but can be distressing to the individual. If someone's mind has regressed back a decade and they are certain it is 2005 because that is where their memory is, insisting it is 2015 will not be something they can connect to in any meaningful way. Do not attempt to "correct" dementia patients when they are wrong about things such as the date or someone's identity. It will only upset them. It is better to affirm and redirect. For example, an individual might make a statement such as "I can't find my purse; someone is breaking into my home at night and moving it." An appropriate response might be something like, "That must be upsetting. I will check on your doors and windows and let's go find your purse." Validate the feeling behind the false perception by saying "I will look into it, or check on that" but take the initial problem, the misplaced purse, and focus on that.

Alzheimer's can affect taste and smell, so food may not be appetizing anymore and utensils might be confusing. There are many great tips online which can enhance mealtime's success such as focusing on dining atmosphere, simplicity and size of meal and table settings, and creating a meal time free of distractions and overwhelming activities.

Even though you don't want to overstimulate the person with dementia, you still want them to have some activities throughout their day. Try to help them engage in things they are still able to do and that they have done for most of their lives, so they are not having to try to utilize their short-term memory. Socializing with one person or a few people is a good activity, if they have enjoyed doing this in the past. There will come a time where they can't do an activity of interest any longer, but there may be ways to modify the activity to still make it possible for them to take part in.

Many caregivers find that when they start caring for someone with dementia, they meet resistance on matters such as bathing and dressing. Some of this may be par for the course, but some of it could be fixed by a simple study of what that individual's routines were before he or she fell ill. I heard a story once about a woman in assisted living who would fight her CNAs tooth and nail each night after dinner when they tried to bathe her. A quick inquiry yielded the fact that for her entire life she had always bathed after breakfast each morning. The staff switched the schedule and the patient was then content with the bathing routine.

At some point a dementia patient will need 24-hour supervision. This can be done in the home by family members and home health aides or in a long-term care facility. Moving a loved one to a facility can be a very difficult decision, but often it provides the only truly safe environment. Many facilities specialize in making their environment more comfortable and appropriately stimulating than a home environment. It's worth pointing out that an individual suffering from dementia may at some point be happier in a facility dedicated to their needs and away from hectic goings-on of a modern era household. Dementia is a progressive disease. As with many other medical conditions, family members cannot be expected to be able to provide all of the care adequate to supporting a loved one who is suffering.

Alzheimer's is a lethal disease. Although many elders with Alzheimer's have one or more other serious health conditions, those may not wind up causing death. If an elder with AD manages to continue living through various conditions with the help of medications, for instance, they will indeed eventually die from Alzheimer's.

The stage of the Alzheimer's disease process that typically causes death is the loss of ability to swallow. No food, drink nor most medications can be ingested, either at all or without causing "aspiration." Aspiration is when the ability to swallow is impeded, and food or drink winds up going into the lungs and not the stomach, frequently resulting in a life-threatening lung infection. All of the body's muscle actions are directed from the brain. We use muscles to swallow. Imagine a brain that includes a lot of plaques, tangles and dead cells. Then imagine how hard it would be for a message "took bite of dinner" to reach the right part of the brain intact, and then for the brain to then send another message to the throat muscles: "perform swallowing maneuvers."

Even the most basic and inherent tasks we do require a signal from the brain. A brain signal trying to reach point B from A in the brain of someone with Alzheimer's will find an increasingly difficult terrain, frequently blocked off, or re-routed, or in need of a highway sized neuro-transmitter, when all it finds to take is a small bumpy road. It is easy to see how Alzheimer's is in fact a lethal disease.

ELDER ABUSE AND NEGLECT

Elderly persons without at least one close-by family member or a network of friends or groups such as fellow churchgoers, who will visit or call frequently, are especially vulnerable to abuse.

Physical abuse. Financial abuse. Psychological abuse. Sexual abuse. Neglect.

Terrible things can happen to the elderly in their own homes as well as in facilities which exist to care for them. A recent edition of the National Academy of Elder Law Attorneys (NAELA) Journal reports horrendous results of a study conducted by the National Council on Elder Abuse (NCEA) directed by the Administration on Aging (AoA). Examples appear below. Utilizing some of the planning opportunities discussed in this book is essential to preventing abuse. But such planning is not, of itself, sufficient in all cases. Having a "second eye" on situations in which the elderly reside, whether in their own homes or in care facilities, is the single most effective abuse preventative.

Studies have reported that between 2 million and 5 million elders are abused or severely neglected each year. The NCEA estimated that for every incident actually reported, thirteen more such incidents go unreported to authorities.

Physical Abuse

If an elderly person in your life frequently appears with bruises, pay attention. The victim might emphatically deny the abuse. The elderly person might be too frightened of her abuser to tell you the truth and may insist that she simply bumped into a door or fell. If you can, document the bruising with photographs. One set of bruises arguably can result from accidental causes, maybe even two. But if you spot a pattern, strongly consider reporting the incidents, together with your photos, to your local Adult Protective Services (APS), discussed below.

When abuse or neglect is suspected in a facility such as a nursing home, contact the ombudsman for that facility. However, most abuse is committed by family members, including spouses and adult children. The abuser is often the primary caregiver. Many abusers have little education and minimal coping skills. Many were abused as children. The proclivity to abuse is very often exacerbated by drug and alcohol abuse.

Physical abuse happens in nursing homes, too. In one incident, a nurse's aide repeatedly hit and punched her patient on and around her face and arms. When asked, the patient denied that she had been hit. She was terrified that she would receive even worse treatment if she "told on" her abuser.

Such abuse would be far less likely if the victim had someone monitoring her care. Usually a monitor would be a family member who lives nearby. When family monitors travel out of town for more than a week or so, they might want to consider hiring a geriatric care management agency to make unscheduled visits to the nursing home.

Most of the staff serving nursing home patients are devoted to their profession. Nursing home abuse correlates with low staffing, poor management systems, low wages and failure to conduct criminal background checks.

If your loved-one is at home, consider a "nanny cam" with a video feed you can monitor when you choose. Alerting aides who are assisting an elder in the home that there is a camera there, to keep tabs on a parent's health, or detect falls if they are alone, can assure an honest, motivated individual intent on doing a good job.

Financial Abuse

Ms. Johnson answered her doorbell to find a pleasant looking man on her porch. She was still living independently even though she was beginning to experience some problems with memory and comprehension.

The man explained that he was a landscaper and was on his way home from working at the home of one of her neighbors, whose name sounded familiar. While driving by, he said, he had noticed that some of her trees had dangerously overhanging branches. They could block the windows of passing cars and even break off and injure someone. He said he could have his crew come out the next day to take care of the trees. She agreed. He asked her for a check for $10,000. She gave it to him. She never saw him again. When a family member noticed the payment, Ms. Johnson became defensive and would not discuss it.

Unfortunately, it may not be surprising that the financial fiduciary, such as a POA or even a court-appointed conservator of the victim, can be the perpetrator of financial abuse. Some abusers are family members who coerce their elderly relatives into signing large checks – or simply forge them.

Elderly people should give powers of attorney to those they trust. Powers of attorney are among the most useful tools available to help elderly people extend their years of independent living. But not all attorneys-in-fact, or POAs, have the integrity with which they are credited. POAs, especially adult children, often use their authority to convert their loved one's money to their own use. This abuse is often not discovered until after the victim's death, when others, such as siblings of the fiduciary adult child, discover that mom's or dad's estate has been looted.

Neglect

One NAELA Journal article reported on one especially horrific example of neglect. A man supposedly caring for his father left his father without food or water for days because he didn't want his father to emit odors during the visit of an expected guest. Dad was found dead on a mattress which had rotted to the springs from constant wetness. He had large, bedsores resulting from dehydration, malnutrition and severe neglect.

Neglect can also occur in even the best nursing homes. A client of the law firm where I worked had reported the wonderful care her husband was receiving at a nursing home. He had Alzheimer's Disease. She visited him every day and knew all the staff. One day she called our office in tears. She had broken her hip several months earlier, undergone rehab and was now able to get around again on her own. Her first stop was the nursing home. She hadn't seen her husband in months.

As she approached his room, one of the aides who remembered her told her that her husband had been moved to the room at the end of the hall. She headed that way. As she approached his doorway, she could smell his unchanged incontinence pad. His hair was dirty and greasy, his skin dry and flaky. She was horrified. The high quality care this client had originally observed was not due to the stellar performance of the nursing home per se, it was due to the fact that her husband was visited daily by someone who was paying attention to his care. With the client no longer around to notice, her husband's care dropped to the bottom of the priority list.

Being visited by someone who is paying attention is the single most important factor in receiving the highest quality of care available in a nursing home or other residential facility. Where possible, family members should divvy up a visiting schedule that is unpredictable. The elderly resident may not even be cognitively aware that they're there, but the staff is. Out-of-town family members can contact the patient's church, synagogue or mosque to see if there are volunteers available to visit nursing home patients. Some community groups also sponsor volunteer visitors programs.

A more costly option is for out-of-town family members to share the cost of retaining a professional geriatric care manager (GCM). GCMs often monitor the quality of care of a number of patients in a nursing home. The patient's care is assured; the family is reassured. See http://www.aginglifecare.org.

Long-Term Care Ombudsman

Long-term care ombudsman programs are operated in each state under the auspices of the Long-Term Care Ombudsman Program (LTCOP) through states' Aging Departments, Area Agencies on Aging and other organizations. An ombudsman is an important part of care in nursing homes.

If you suspect your loved one is experiencing abuse or neglect in a nursing home, assisted living facility or other adult residential care facility, an ombudsman can receive and take steps to resolve complaints. An ombudsman is familiar with the laws governing long-term care and can be very a valuable advocate for patient rights, as well as mediating disputes between residents, families and facilities.

Every community is required by state regulation to post information and make readily available how to contact the Ombudsman. Check online at http://ltcombudsman.org/ or call Eldercare Locator at 1-800-677-1116 and ask for the local Long-term Care Ombudsman Program.

Preventing Abuse and Enhancing Quality of Life

Individuals with loving, honest and geographically proximate families will be the least likely to suffer abuse and neglect. Experience also tells us that well-to-do individuals who plan ahead using trusts and powers of attorney, wherein more than one set of eyes are on both the incapacitated person's money and his or her personal care, will also likely be well and safely cared for in their final days.

But having enough money for the very best care plan available does not guarantee safety and comfort in old age. Just look at the case of Brooke Astor, the hotel heiress, philanthropist and socialite. She had the money but not the plan. Her son fired her devoted staff members. He removed her from the home she loved. He looted her estate. He went to prison. But his punishment doesn't restore how Ms. Astor could have lived her last days.

Compare Brooke Astor's last days with those of Rose Kennedy who died at home at 104, and with those of Ms. Kennedy's son-in-law, Sargent Shriver, an Alzheimer's victim. Ms. Kennedy and Ambassador Shriver spent their last years in their own homes, surrounded by loved ones, physically safe, cared for in comfort. They probably had the right legal structures in place, but they might not even have needed them; they had good family.

Adult Protective Services (APS)

If you witness or suspect abuse, neglect, or even self-neglect of a vulnerable elderly adult, you should contact your local office of Adult Protective Services (APS), which can then move forward with an investigation. Each state has its own APS programs. Unfortunately, APS is often met with denial by the alleged victim. If the victim seems lucid, there is very little that APS can do except wait for a more severe incident which will justify intervention over the objection of the victim. The tension between preventing abuse of the elderly, on the one hand, and respecting their rights to privacy and self-determination, on the other, is one of the reasons issues of abuse and neglect are so pervasive.

For a state directory of helplines, hotlines and other elder abuse prevention programs, visit the website of the National Center on Elder Abuse at https://ncea.acl.gov/resources/state.html where you will find a directory of APS contact numbers by state. The National Adult Protective Services Association can also provide information at http://www.napsa-now.org/.

HEALTHCARE DIRECTIVES: IT'S YOUR DECISION

The three legally binding planning documents that pertain to your health are:

- Healthcare Power of Attorney (HPOA),
- Living Will, and
- Do Not Resuscitate Order (DNR).

The first two, HPOA and Living Will, can be found in one document called an Advance Medical Directive (AMD).

Some states have enacted statutes authorizing a document that *combines* the Healthcare POA and the Living Will. These combined documents have made expressing your medical wishes much more convenient. If you have an AMD, that one document will include within it two sections that traditionally existed as separate documents- The HPOA and the Living Will. If you have two documents titled HPOA and Living Will, that is OK, they are still valid. Whether you have one AMD or two separate documents, the context is:

- To appoint an agent to act for you in matters regarding health (HPOA)
- To direct medical professionals in matters regarding a terminal condition (LIVING WILL).

A Do Not Resuscitate Order, unlike an AMD, can only be obtained from your medical doctor, not an attorney. In the past, there was no need to designate a person to decide your health care decisions when there was no such thing as living in a vegetative state, or living for years with illnesses like Alzheimer's. People just did not live that long, and we did not have the medical machinery to keep us alive, at least for very long, through incapacitation.

Estate Planning for regular people became a "new age" necessity by the 1980's.

Many of us remember Terry Schiavo. This was the case of a woman in an irreversible vegetative state who was the focus of a long-term court battle between her husband and her parents over whether life-prolonging measures should be continued. State statutes now are in place which determine who can make medical decisions for you *if you have not* appointed someone through an advance medical directive document. However, family dynamics can be complicated, and the person designated by statute to make decisions for you might not be the same person you would have chosen. We will never know what Terry Schiavo would have wanted for herself. You have the power to choose.

An Advance Medical Directive will have a section in which you appoint somebody to be your Healthcare Power of Attorney (HPOA). Most people appoint family members or close friends, although you can appoint anyone you feel can follow through on your medical directive if you are unable to communicate an informed decision.

Healthcare Power of Attorney (HPOA)

A Healthcare Power of Attorney (HPOA) can act for you when you cannot communicate an informed decision on your own, either because you cannot physically communicate in any way, even by blinking an eye, or because you cannot formulate an informed decision due to severe cognitive impairment. An HPOA document usually states that if an attending physician and one other physician or licensed psychologist deem a person unable to communicate an informed decision, the physician and other health care workers will follow the direction of the Healthcare Power of Attorney regarding the patient's treatment. The power of this document eliminates the need to have a public guardianship hearing in which you and/or others might engage in stressful, wrenching arguments about what decision is the right one for you or your loved one.

Depending on a specific state's rules, the HPOA document can be narrow or *limited* - granting an HPOA for a single event such as surgery, or *broad* - deciding all "healthcare-related" decisions for you including signing a Do Not Resuscitate Order (DNR).

HPOAs originally applied only to medical decisions, such as consenting to surgery on your behalf. Most states have broadened the application of "medical" directives so that an HPOA can also make decisions about such things as admission to assisted living or nursing home facilities. These were not traditionally seen as being "medical" decisions per se, but can be very valuable as a practical matter. Newer documents will typically use the term "healthcare" decisions instead of "medical" decisions.

An unusual and controversial subject which can also be put to rest by the HPOA document is a determination by you about who should be permitted to visit you when you are a patient. Settling the legal authority of the HPOA in this regard can head off otherwise explosive family controversies. The default position in most states is that an HPOA cannot restrict who can visit a patient in a healthcare facility unless a patient, through their HPOA document, specifically grants that right to the HPOA.

It is crucial to discuss your desires about your healthcare wishes with your HPOA. The HPOA is supposed to be acting for you, as you would act yourself, and not insert his or her own wishes. The HPOA cannot do this job if he or she does not know your wishes. Your HPOA must also have no reservations, religious or otherwise, about honoring your wishes; finding out in advance could be very important.

EXAMPLE:
- Dad appoints daughter as HPOA, when he is 85 and feeling fine.
- Dad decides to go jet skiing at the local inlet. While doing so he collides with another jet skier and is taken to the hospital unconscious.

Dad needs surgery. There are pros and cons regarding the treatment options. One is to amputate the leg; another is to try to save it. Both have risks and repercussions and someone needs to make a decision. Dad is unconscious and unable to make this decision, so it falls on his daughter, the HPOA.

Living Will

A Living Will is a document signed by you which states what your wishes would be if you were dying and further treatment would serve only to prolong the dying process. Living Wills usually specify that you wish to receive all medications and procedures required to keep you comfortable and pain free, but not treatment to try to cure you. Note that a Living Will has nothing to do with a regular will (Last Will and Testament), and it is *not* a living trust.

The Living Will got that name because just as with a regular will, where you direct what you want to be done with your belongings, a Living Will directs what you want done with your "self" when you are close to death. The Living Will document speaks directly from you to medical personnel when you are in a terminal condition, with no HPOA intermediary.

If you have both an HPOA and a Living Will document, the Living Will trumps the power of the HPOA when the circumstances of your health and condition listed on the Living Will are in effect.

This can alleviate the stressful burden on the Healthcare Power of Attorney if he or she were asked whether or not the medical team should keep you on life support when there's virtually no chance of your recovery.

These documents were not readily accepted by the medical community until the 1990s because they seemed to conflict with the Hippocratic Oath to do no harm. Doctors felt obligated to do everything medically necessary to keep a patient alive. Before Living Wills gained wide acceptance, attorneys would threaten to sue doctors who refused to follow the directives that a person had signed. Doctors seem to have shifted their opinions as to what constitutes "do no harm", given the modern ability to keep people alive when their quality of life is very low. Now, under applicable Medicare law, hospitals are required to ask patients if they have an Advance Medical Directive (AMD), and to offer them a generic Living Will form if the patient has no AMD.

EXAMPLE:
- Dad is now 95 and has Alzheimer's Disease. He is unable to eat or drink. He will not live long unless he is given IV fluids and a feeding tube for nutrition.
- Dad's <u>Living Will </u>says that he does not want to prolong his dying process by "invasive treatments" in order to be kept alive, and it also says he wants to be made as comfortable as possible until he dies.
- Daughter will likely consult with hospice at this time. She will be relieved of the burden of feeling like she had to be the one to decide Dad's fate, because Dad made that decision for himself when he signed the Living Will years earlier.

The Five Wishes

As of publication of this book, forty two of the fifty states accept outright a document called *The Five Wishes* as a legal and valid Advance Medical Directive document. (It was written with the help of the American Bar Association's Commission on Law & Aging.) It is a document that you can download from the internet and fill out yourself. It is a version of an Advance Medical Directive, combining features of both a Healthcare POA and a Living Will. This document is typically accepted in the medical community and can also work very well as a starting point for family discussions concerning individualized decisions about treatment you may or may not want. Some of the details about the wishes may go beyond what you would find in a legal document, such as whether you want music playing in your hospital room or prayer at your bedside.

The five wishes are:

- Which person you want to make healthcare decisions for you when you can't;
- The kind of medical treatment you want or don't want;
- How comfortable you want to be;
- How you want people to treat you;
- What you want your loved ones to know.

For more information, visit www.agingwithdignity.org.

Do Not Resuscitate Order (DNR)

A Do Not Resuscitate Order (DNR) is used when a patient who is already ill or is near death has an emergency situation, usually from cardiac or respiratory arrest. This document is signed at a doctor's office or in a hospital. There is an effort underway by some groups to rename the Do Not Resuscitate order (DNR) as the Allow Natural Death order (AND). A DNR is obtained by a doctor, not a lawyer, because a consult with a doctor is necessary to determine whether the individual has a condition such that it makes sense for them to choose not to be resuscitated. If a totally healthy 40-year-old mother of three children asked a doctor for a DNR, the doctor would likely refer the woman to a mental health professional rather than sign a DNR order for her. A 90-year-old with a diagnosis of advanced dementia would likely be considered a solid candidate for a DNR order.

People who are extremely ill and/or fragile, and are living in their own homes, place their DNR in a conspicuous place, such as on the refrigerator. If an ambulance is called, the medical personnel will likely look there to see if CPR, defibrillation, or other treatments should be started. A person may also opt to have a DNR bracelet.

Imagine you are terminally ill with a few weeks to live, which likely will be physically painful or uncomfortable. If you suffer an emergency, such as a heart attack, your caregiver may still call 911, but the paramedics can determine whether you would benefit from resuscitation (whether they would normally start it upon arrival) and then honor the DNR by not administering it. Should you come to on your own, or have other non-life threatening medical issues, the paramedics may be of assistance.

Many patients are incapacitated at the time immediately preceding their death. That means they are unable to make decisions for themselves. Like a Living Will, a DNR trumps any direction from a Healthcare Power of Attorney because it speaks directly to medical personnel. Patients who are being cared for at home while in a terminal condition often notify their local emergency medical personnel that they have a DNR in effect - or their HPOA or family member can make such notification for the patient.

In a growing number of states, there is a "newer version" of what a DNR document aims to allow patients to decide. It is called a POLST. (See below).

The Physician Orders for Life Sustaining Treatment

The Physician Orders for Life Sustaining Treatment Document is most often referred to as the POLST form. It was developed in order to provide patients with more control over their healthcare in the final stages of life. It is not meant to, nor does it, take the place of a Health Care Power of Attorney or a Living Will. Rather it acts as a supplement to those forms.

POLST is not appropriate for everyone. It is for patients with serious illnesses or frailty with an expectation determined by a physician that death is more likely than not to occur within a year. It allows patients, in consultation with their health care providers, to determine what treatments they do or do not want, taking into account their personal beliefs and current health status.

The form is completed after a patient has had a discussion with their healthcare provider regarding their diagnosis, prognosis and treatment options, including life-sustaining treatment. The patient and the healthcare provider then reach an informed decision together regarding desired treatment based on the patient's values, beliefs and goals for care.

The form does in fact require that ordinary measures to improve the patient's comfort always be provided. The form is signed by the health care professionals who are accountable for the medical orders.

Other names for this form are Medical Orders for Scope of Treatment (MOST), Physician Orders for Scope of Treatment (POST) and Medical Orders for Life-Sustaining Treatment (MOLST).

HOSPICE

Hospice was traditionally thought of as a place or facility where terminally ill patients received end-of-life care. However, hospice is actually a type of care which can be received either in a patient's own home or in a facility like assisted living or nursing home. Free-standing hospice facilities are another alternative for care. However, depending on your location, the availability of a room in such a facility may be nonexistent.

The vast majority of hospice patients are cared for in a home setting, either their own home or that of a relative or friend.

Patients receive treatment for pain, anxiety and discomfort; they do not receive treatment that is aimed at curing or treating their terminal condition. Hospice care may also provide treatments that have traditionally been regarded as curative, including radiation therapy or antibiotics, if they are administered to improve "quality of life" as distinct from trying to cure the patient. Such non-curative treatments are commonly called "palliative care." Palliative care is also utilized by non-terminal patients who have long, debilitating illnesses.

With practices largely defined by Medicare, hospice care is made available to patients of any age with any terminal prognosis who are medically certified to have fewer than six months to live. This six-month certification can be renewed. More than one-third of dying Americans utilize this service. Skilled medical hospice care is covered 100% by Medicare if you are over 65 and in a facility, and almost 100% for the hospice portion of your care if you receive hospice care at home.

As for actual medical costs, such as injections by a registered nurse, the medications and RN visits themselves, any helpful equipment such as a lift to help the patient out of bed and other specified care will be covered by the Hospice benefit under Medicare Part A. Most state Medicaid programs and private health insurance plans also cover hospice care. Hospice personnel, such as registered nurses, are on-call 24/7.

For those who are younger with non-Medicare insurance policies, check on your individual plan for coverage details.

Care at home presupposes that you have a primary caregiver. Hospice does not pay such caregivers, but will cover respite services. (See below). A home health aide can be hired by you or your family to serve as a primary caregiver or as a helper to the family caregiver. The cost of a home health aide is about $20 per hour depending on where you live.

If you live in as assisted living or nursing home, the regular monthly fees would still apply even though hospice coverage is taking care of the "extra" services.

If a hospice patient experiences an event that would usually prompt a call to 911, the caregiver would instead call the 24-hour hospice number. Hospice patients are not generally taken to the hospital; they are treated in their homes by physicians and nurses. An example of going to the hospital while under hospice care would be if a patient fell and needed stiches to stop bleeding.

There are four primary levels of Hospice care. The level of care determines what services will be paid for by hospice insurance coverage:

Routine Care is provided when a patient is receiving hospice care at home or in a facility and symptoms are under control. Insurance will likely cover regular visits by an RN or LPN, a social worker or a doctor, as well as an occasional visit by an HHA or CNA to help with things like bathing.

General Inpatient Care is that which is provided when a patient is receiving hospice in a facility such as a stand-alone hospice facility, or a hospital, because symptoms are not under control. Again, skilled care for nursing visits is covered, but regular facility costs will still be out-of-pocket.

Continuous Care is provided when a patient's symptoms are out of control and hospice must provide continuous care either at home or on an inpatient basis at a facility. At this level, the presence of an HHA or CNA may be covered by Medicare Hospice Benefits.

Respite Care is extra care that is provided to the patient to give family members a break in order to rest or take off for an emergency. Respite care can be provided up to five days at a time, but the five days must be continuous. Therefore, hospice coverage will pay for an HHA or CNA to be present with the patient at this level of care *in a qualified facility.*

The fact that a patient qualifies medically for hospice does not mean that a family should feel compelled to request it. If the family and patient are satisfied with their current care plan, there may be no reason to change it. There are, however, certain circumstances when hospice would be highly recommended. These would include situations where the patient does "qualify" for hospice care and, for instance, has a pressure ulcer (also known as a bedsore) anywhere on their body or is having difficulty swallowing. In these cases hospice care would be beneficial for the patient's comfort if brought in whether they are at home or in a facility. When hospice is requested, be sure that the forms you have signed are for actual hospice care and not just palliative care. Once hospice care has been put in place, the family will be assigned a physician who will be overseeing the care who may consult with your primary care doctor if you have one. Therefore, it is important to remember to call the hospice doctor first rather than the patient's primary/former physician with any questions or concerns because the hospice doctor is in a position to respond quickly at any time of day or night.

CONCLUSION

For those now in their 50s and up, most of the programs, services, facilities and other options discussed in this book should still be available for you when your turn comes.

But we are an aging nation. Although the total fertility rate in the U.S. is about equal to the "replacement" rate of 2.1 children per woman, that rate is expected to decline.

Lower fertility rates will mean that fewer young people in the workforce will be paying taxes to support those who have retired. And fewer will be available to underwrite the potentially staggering costs of long-term care for our longer-lived, aging citizens.

Nevertheless, I am an optimist. People in 1900 could never have imagined that a large vehicle could fly hundreds of passengers through the air or that people could talk to others anywhere in the world by simply holding a small rectangular instrument in the palm of their hands. They couldn't imagine satellites, antibiotics or flat screen TVs. What types of care will our then-aging grandchildren have?

I hope that when our grandchildren become elderly, a book like this one can help to guide them to tomorrow's solutions. In the meantime, I hope that this book will be helpful to those affected by the realities of today and the near future.

Most of all, realize that you have the power to make choices now for your future self.

ACRONYM APPENDIX

A&A: Aid and Attendance, in context of Veterans Benefits

AAA: Area Agency on Aging

AAMVA: American Association of Motor Vehicle Administrators

AARP: American Association of Retired Persons

AD: Alzheimer's Disease

ADA: Americans with Disabilities Act (of 1990)

ADEAR Center: Alzheimer's Disease Education and Referral Center

ADLs: Activities of Daily Living such as bathing, toileting etc.

ALF: Assisted Living Facility

AMD: Advance Medical Directive.

AMS: Amyotrophic-Lateral-Sclerosis, aka Lou Gehrig's Disease

AND: Allow Natural Death order (alternate name for DNR)

AoA: Administration on Aging (part of the Social Security Administration)

APS: Adult Protective Services

CCRC: Continuing Care Retirement Community

CD: Certificate of Deposit

CFP: Certified Financial Planner

CMC: abbreviation for Certified Care Manager

CMN: Certificate of Medical Necessity

CMS: Centers for Medicare and Medicaid Services

CNA: Certified Nursing Assistant

CPA: Certified Public Accountant

CPWA: Certified Private Wealth Advisor

CS: Community Spouse

CSA: Certified Senior Advisor

CSPRA: Community Spouse Protected Resource Amount

CSRA: Community Spouse Resource Allowance

DHS: Department of Human Services

DLB: Dementia with Lewy Bodies

DME: Durable Medical Equipment

DMV: Department of Motor Vehicles

DNR: Do Not Resuscitate

DPOA: Durable Power of Attorney, also "DPA"

DSS: Department of Social Services

EJA: Elder Justice Act

ESRD: End Stage Renal Disease

FTD: Frontotemporal Dementia

GCM: Geriatric Care Manager

HB: Housebound Benefit in the context of Veterans Benefits

HECM: Home Equity Conversion Mortgage ("Reverse Mortgage")

HHA: Home Health Aide

HMO: Health Maintenance Organization

HPOA: Healthcare Power of Attorney

ILIT: Irrevocable Life Insurance Trust

IRA: Individual Retirement Account

IS: Institutionalized Spouse

IVAP: Income for VA Purposes

JTEN: Joint Tenants

JTWROS: Joint Tenants with Right of Survivorship

LCSW: Licensed Clinical Social Worker

LTC: Long-Term Care

LTCI: Long-Term Care Insurance

LTCOP: Long-Term Care Ombudsman Program

MAPR: Maximum Annual Pension Rate

MCI: Mild Cognitive Impairment

MMMNA: Minimum (or Maximum) Monthly Maintenance Needs Allowance

MOW: Meals on Wheels

MOLST: Medical Orders for Life-Sustaining Treatment

MOST: Medical Orders for Scope of Treatment

MSW: Master's in Social Work

NAELA: National Academy of Elder Law Attorneys

NCEA: National Council on Elder Abuse

NH: Nursing Home

NHTSA: National Highway Traffic Safety Agency

NIA: National Institute on Aging

NORC: Naturally Occurring Retirement Communities

OASDI: Old Age Survivors and Disability Insurance

OT: Occupational Therapist

PART A: Medicare Part A covers hospitals and care in SNFs

PART B: Medicare Part B covers doctors and out-patient tests

Part C: Medicare Part C (aka Medicare Advantage) is an HMO-type substitute for Parts A, B, D and Medigap

PART D: Medicare Part D covers prescriptions

PDD: Parkinson's Disease with Dementia

POA: Power of Attorney - technically the document; in practical usage, it is also the agent

POD: Payable on Death

POLST: Physician Orders for Life-Sustaining Treatment

PIA: Primary Insurance Amount for Social Security purposes

PPACA: Patient Protection and Affordable Care Act

RMD: Required Minimum Distribution from IRA account

RN: Registered Nurse

ROTH IRA: IRA in which contributions are taxable but payments coming out are not

SNF: Skilled Nursing Facility (pronounced "sniff")

SNT: Special Needs Trust (pronounced "snit")

SSA: Social Security Administration

SSDI: Social Security Disability Insurance (or income)

SSI: Supplemental Security Income

ST: Speech Therapist

T/E: Tenants by the Entirety (for married couples only)

TOD: Transfer on Death

TOP: Treasury Offset Program

UME: Unreimbursed Medical Expense in context of VA benefits

UPOAA: Uniform Power of Attorney Act

UTI: Urinary Tract Infection

VA: U.S. Department of Veterans Affairs (formerly the Veterans Administration)

VBA: Veterans Benefits Administration

VSA: Veterans Services Alliance

WCVO: Written Confirmation of Verbal Order

WEP: Windfall Elimination Provision

401(k) (aka 401K): Retirement plan to which both employers and employees contribute

(d)(4)(A): US Code subsection that authorizes self-funded "Medicaid payback SNTs"

****

CPSIA information can be obtained
at www.ICGtesting.com
Printed in the USA
BVHW01s0156310718
523149BV00010B/108/P